"This is a quiet memoir, more f
companionship than autobiogra
her story, showing beauty to be the heroine and truth, the bulwark. We need more stories like this in the world, more humans willing to carry their readers with them on their own journey through the dark nights we all live and sometimes love and will someday leave."

Lore Ferguson Wilbert, author of *Handle with Care: How Jesus Redeems the Power of Touch in Life and Ministry*

"From inside the darkness, Sarah Clarkson writes of a light that shines. She pulls the curtain back on her struggle with a particular kind of mental illness, offering not simply a theology of suffering and hope but a portrait of God's grace in the midst of our brokenness. Beautiful in its prose and in the love it reveals, this book is a balm to a world weary of evil."

Glenn Packiam, associate senior pastor, New Life Church; author of *Blessed Broken Given*

"I read Sarah Clarkson's book through grateful tears. When we are weighed down by painful questions, it is stories we need most, not answers. Sarah bravely and generously shares her own particular story in a book that is filled to the brim with truth, goodness, and beauty. Sarah has a gift for making abstract ideas real and tangible. I didn't read about hope in these pages. Instead, I was offered it."

Christie Purifoy, author of *Placemaker* and *Roots and Sky*

"Sarah Clarkson has risked a great deal in writing this book. She has loved her reader enough to tell the unvarnished, complicated truth about a tormented life. In exploring her dark battles with OCD, she lays down her life so that others might live. The space she creates here is so intimate, so honest, that I found myself barely breathing as I read. The power of pure authenticity sits in these pages, and God met me in that bareness. Clarkson does not offer a shallow, escapist treatise on beauty but a raw glimpse into the cosmic battle between goodness and evil—through the lens of a single trembling mortal soul, learning to hope and believe while living dead center in the war zone."

Rebecca K. Reynolds, author of *Courage, Dear Heart*

"Few of us can return from the edge of the abyss in our own selves; fewer still are those who are able to recount at all what we have seen there. But rarer still is the one who can retell it truthfully while casting the shadows there into light. Sarah Clarkson has written that tale with courage, grace, and defiant hope. If you have ever needed to hear why beauty heals the brokenhearted, here is the telling. This is the book I have been waiting for my whole life. It may be for you too."

Lancia E. Smith, founder and executive director of the Cultivating Project

"*This Beautiful Truth* is not only a beautifully written book; it is also an incredibly brave book—brave in its determination to stare down the darkness and bear witness to the light that tells a truer story, and brave also in its raw vulnerability. By chronicling her harrowing private battle with mental illness and its attendant feelings of guilt, shame, confusion, and doubt, Sarah Clarkson has cracked open her heart on paper so that others with broken hearts might find echoes of their own pain and know they are not alone."

Jennifer Trafton, author of *Henry and the Chalk Dragon* and *The Rise and Fall of Mount Majestic*

"Here is theology grounded in experience. In her beautiful and fluent prose, Sarah weaves a message of hope amidst brokenness that lifts our horizons. This book will open your eyes to beauty in myriad ways that are both breathtaking and mysterious in their power to heal."

Rev. Dr. Liz Hoare, director of welfare, pastoral care, and spirituality at Wycliffe Hall, Oxford this beautiful truth

this
beautiful
truth

How God's Goodness Breaks
into Our Darkness

SARAH CLARKSON

BakerBooks
a division of Baker Publishing Group
Grand Rapids, Michigan

© 2021 by Sarah Clarkson

Published by Baker Books
a division of Baker Publishing Group
PO Box 6287, Grand Rapids, MI 49516-6287
www.bakerbooks.com

Printed in the United States of America

Library of Congress Cataloging-in-Publication Data
Names: Clarkson, Sarah (Editor for Whole Heart Press), author.
Title: This beautiful truth : how God's goodness breaks into our darkness / Sarah Clarkson.
Description: Grand Rapids, Michigan : Baker Books, a division of Baker Publishing Group, [2021]
Identifiers: LCCN 2020056158 | ISBN 9781540901729 (casebound) | ISBN 9781540900517 (paperback) | ISBN 9781493428748 (ebook)
Subjects: LCSH: Clarkson, Sarah (Editor for Whole Heart Press) | Christian biography—United States. | Christian women—United States—Biography. | Mental health—Religious aspects—Christianity. | Mental illness—Religious aspects—Christianity.
Classification: LCC BR1725.C5125 A3 2021 | DDC 283.092 [B]—dc23
LC record available at https://lccn.loc.gov/2020056158

This publication is intended to provide helpful and informative material on the subjects addressed. Readers should consult their personal health professionals before adopting any of the suggestions in this book or drawing inferences from it. The author and publisher expressly disclaim responsibility for any adverse effects arising from the use or application of the information contained in this book.

Published in association with The Bindery Agency, www.TheBindery Agency.com

21 22 23 24 25 26 27   7 6 5 4 3 2 1

For Thomas,
my eucatastrophe.

Contents

Contents

Foreword

I had a bit of a sense of déjà vu while reading this book. Every year at Wycliffe, we hold a creative writing competition, named after Frederick Buechner and funded by the Frederick Buechner Center. And every year that Sarah was a student at Wycliffe, one entry would jump out at me as of an outstandingly impressive quality and depth.

I had the same experience when marking academic papers. We have a policy of double-blind marking at Oxford, which is meant to ensure that the markers never know whose script they are marking. The sheer quality of writing that confronted the marker of Sarah's papers made that well nigh impossible!

The same quality of writing and depth of feeling pulsate from the pages of this book. It is a beautifully written book about the power (and ultimate source and goal) of beauty. There are few more important—or urgent—topics. The church has rightly proclaimed God as Love—the understanding of God as Trinity has enabled and compelled it to see the giving and receiving of love as essential to God's very being. The church has rightly proclaimed Christ as the Truth—the one whose utter freedom from the distorting effects of self-promotion enables him to see things as they truly are and, indeed, enables all things to be what they are. (All self-promotion warps both the self and all those with whom the self comes into contact, squeezing them out of their proper shape; that which is free from all self-promotion does the opposite.)

But the church has largely forgotten that God is also Beauty. It has ceased to be the patron of the arts that it once was. It has assumed that ugly buildings can proclaim God as well as beautiful ones can—or, worse still, has failed to notice or mind the difference.

And the result is that when people have had an experience of Beauty and been moved and healed and transformed by it, they have not known it was God they have encountered. Our failure to proclaim God as Beauty has deprived our generation of one of the key codes that might have helped them to decipher the meaning of their own lives. Our failure to proclaim God as Beauty has largely removed one of the most important ways in which people recognize God's enriching, deepening, humanizing, and healing presence in their lives and respond to it.

This warm and radiant book unpolemically corrects that deficiency. It testifies to the power of Beauty. It speaks the name of Beauty. It sings the praise of Beauty. And it does so beauteously.

Beauty is scarce in so much of our landscape. But we are still made for it. We still need it. We still crave it. We still respond to it when we come across it. This book will help us to know that experience for what it is—not just aesthetic but relational. Not an encounter with something but with Someone. Hence the warmth.

The very title of this book reminds us that beauty and truth are not different things. Truth is beautiful and beauty is truthful because they are both immediate aspects of the Love upon which all things depend. Therefore, our lived proclamation of God needs to be truthful, loving, and beautiful if it is to act as a pathway.

Because our proclamation of God must be truthful, loving, and beautiful, it must never implicate God in the untruthfulness, hatefulness, and ugliness of evil. It must never attribute evil to the intention of God. As we see in the miracles of Jesus, God is against suffering. In the person of Jesus, he has assaulted it. Whenever we see Jesus and suffering together, we see him undoing it. We therefore have no warrant for saying that suffering is ever divinely desired or intended. Theologically, that impugns the goodness and love of God. Pastorally, that makes God a suffering or grieving person's enemy. Psychologically, it forces us to twist our minds into accepting that bad is actually good. This book is a plea to present God as the healer and never the inflictor of our pain.

It is thus a book of pastoral wisdom and love, of autobiographical honesty and vulnerability, of artistic sensitivity and passion, of human gentleness and compassion. Above all, perhaps, it is a book of wonderful warmth, and it inspires me to greater creativity, homeliness, and holiness in what Sarah calls the ordinary of life.

Michael Lloyd

Beautiful or Broken

The Rival Stories of the World

"Listen to me," cried Syme with extraordinary emphasis. "Shall I tell you the secret of the whole world? It is that we have only known the back of the world. We see everything from behind, and it looks brutal. That is not a tree, but the back of a tree. That is not a cloud, but the back of a cloud. Cannot you see that everything is stooping and hiding a face? If we could only get round in front—"

G. K. Chesterton, *The Man Who Was Thursday*

Swift, swift, the flit and leap of the butterfly and my headlong chase after her through the dry grass in the high summer heat. Again and again I thought my hands would gently close on her fragile wings, but always the little "buckeye" disappeared. I would crouch in wait until suddenly the earth somewhere near me would seem to slip apart in a flash of orange and azure as my butterfly leapt from the ground to lead the chase afresh. I ran breathlessly after, tireless, taut, and wildly joyous in a way that defied my nine-year-old vocabulary to express.

I had butterfly mania that summer. My family had just moved to a new home in the far reaches of Texas Hill Country. We lived with my grandmother on two hundred acres of cedar and dry grass casually named "the ranch" (the name much fancier than the place). In our first days we children had been strictly warned not to venture too casually into the fields, where all sorts of "critturs" awaited us: rattlesnakes and copperheads, fire ants, hornets' nests, and the teensy pests called "chiggers" that had already left angry patterns of crimson and itching bumps across my legs.

I obeyed until early one morning in our first month when I discovered a dewy-winged marvel of a creature in my grand-mother's garden, all midnight black and iridescent blue with circles of white that glimmered up at me like eyes. I ran in fiery excitement to get my grandmother. And "Oh, it's a swal-lowtail," she said nonchalantly—as if this creature, like a tiny seraph or faerie queen from the realm of myth, was a matter of the everyday. She marched inside and pulled an old Audubon guide off the shelf. It became my obsessive study as I immersed myself in the world of tiger and spicebush swallowtails, fritil-laries and buckeyes, painted ladies, and that rare blue ghost, the Diana. The names, the rare, gleaming colors seemed to open an otherworld of beauty that made me hungry for something I couldn't name. That hunger drew me past caution or even guilt (which as a first child I was so very quick to heed) into the crackle and whir of the yellow light, the searing heat, and the grasshopper symphony of the summer fields.

That particular day I didn't even realize how far I'd run as I chased my buckeye through the fields. I was drawn farther and farther up and into the golden world, the next hillock of grass, the next stand of squat, brown cedars. Until my breath ran out. I remember sinking to the dirt then, knees knobbled by the pebbles, laughing after my fifth attempt to catch the little thing. I was delighted in the hunt after that beauty, the way it flashed out, an unexpected grace in the brown landscape, the way it made me hungry and happy all at once. My breath slowed. The pounding of my blood eased in my ears and I sat back on my heels, alert and still.

Abruptly, and more completely than I can describe, my sense of time was suspended as I lifted my face to the great blue dome of the Texas sky, brimmed with the honey-tinged light of late afternoon. The sounds of the earth grew distant, and a quiet came into my mind and body. For one mesmerizing moment I became aware of the personal, present goodness thrumming in every atom of the world around me. I knew that this was the beauty whose presence I yearned to touch in the mystical beauty of those butterfly wings. I knew that I was encountering God. And I knew, with a knowledge as pervasive within me as my own heartbeat, that I was loved, loved, loved.

The next instant the buzz of the cicadas and the far-off cough of a pickup roared back into my ears, and time stomped forward and I was a sunburned little girl with grass stains on her jeans, chasing butterflies. But I felt as if the brown wings of the cosmos itself had fluttered open as I chased the small beauty of the butterfly, and what I glimpsed was the mesmerizing beauty of Love, a beauty stronger and more real than anything else I knew. This, I knew in my bones, is my story.

Until a dark night, probably just a few weeks later though I cannot now exactly remember.

I had been kissed and put to bed as usual by my parents. I lay in the darkness, waiting for the usual descent of sleep. But my brain seemed strangely wired; my thoughts came faster and faster and they began to career toward images of horror that terrified me. My heart beat hard. I closed my eyes, but that was no help. My imagination ran at frenzied speed, peopling the room I couldn't now see with evil shapes and images. I opened my eyes in desperation. But my imagination flung scene after scene into my mind, images that baffle and disgust me to this day.

I still find it hard to write about the obsessive, intrusive images that have plagued me throughout my life and came to me first, as brief portents of a total breaking to come, in that darkness (though I think they had come in dreams before). I tried to describe them to my mom when I was young, but even then I was too ashamed to give full description to the violent, perverted ideas and pictures that came—unbidden, unsought, undreamed of—from out of some void inside my own brain, wrapping themselves around my inner pictures of the people I loved most in the world. I covered my face, trying to physically beat back the thoughts. But I couldn't. I felt attacked and guilty, terrified and contaminated. And in those dark nights, the pervasive reality that suffused my being was my sense of being broken and guilty of my own breaking, attacked and somehow contaminated by my own terror.

The episode I experienced that night in its fullness for the first time was a warning shot by a mind on the edge of breaking. It would be eight more years before I was diagnosed with a lesser-known form of OCD, when stress and hormones complicated my body and triggered the full expression of my mental illness at seventeen. But the absolute nature of that darkness, the caged, sticky sense of having evil resident inside the closed rooms of my own imagination—evil that contaminated everything I loved, that seemed to devour my hope and innocence, that sought to reset the horizons of my identity—that I tasted first as a small child. And in the shadowed agony of those nights in my bed, I immediately knew its radical power, its intended threat to the story told into my being by my recent encounter with beauty.

Even at nine years old, I recognized that the darkness I saw and the despair it worked within me presented a powerful narrative about existence: it closed the horizons of hope by caging me in with fear; it cut me off from relationship as I drew away in shame from others; it told me that the bleak, shattered reality I experienced was the ultimate reality of the world and of my guilty, miserable self. I remember in the days that followed feeling cut off from the beauty—the endless fields, the countless butterflies to be chased—by the grey, dulled sense of the darkness I had tasted and the guilt it birthed in me. I could no longer feel that great, golden heartbeat of Love. I remember the confused, childish grief I felt as I wondered within myself how to tell which potent, insistent narrative was true. And why God didn't come to tell me himself. Thus, in that marvelous and terrifying summer of my little girlhood, I was introduced to the rival stories of the world.

Beautiful or broken? Despair or hope? Evil or love?

I've been trying to answer those questions ever since. I've been trying to decide which story is true. And I think this is the fight to which each of us is called every day of our lives.

For we all experience both perspectives, often from littlest childhood. The story of shattering, of course. We bear within ourselves the narratives of our rejection and disease, our stories marred by loss and struggle. Abandonment, abuse, miscarriage and divorce, tsunamis and unexpected cancer—these are the daily, pervasive, personal realities we taste and touch. And the story they tell us is of a world so evil, so shattered and grieved that we wonder how goodness could ever have been. In the shadow sight it sets upon us, we think of things like beauty or hope, story or song as frivolities that only distract us from the single, great reality of our grief.

The question we have to ask, of course, is where God dwells in the midst of all this sorrow. Faith in a great, untouchable Good is the realm in which we are supposed to find hope for all this fallenness. If we have grown up in some form of the Christian faith, we often have a bone-deep sense that suffering is a test, a season in which we must grip harder to our belief, and for a while, sometimes, that is possible. We may have a vague idea that God is "in control" (whatever we mean by that) so that what happens to us is "his will." We so often confront profound suffering with a list of doctrinal tenets and assertions that are meant, I think, to stave off that yawning terror of inexplicable destruction. We don't want to feel fragile. We don't want to believe that God would let evil happen to us.

And yet he does. Evil in our minds and to our bodies. Evil in the actions of others and the ravages of a disordered cosmos. Evil growing up in our own impulses, our own tangled yearning. And sometimes the evil is so great and the grief so destructive that we are drawn by our pain into a wild, trackless realm where the neat explanations and the trim, sermon-sized assertions we used to keep terror at bay no longer protect us. Like Job, we are drawn into the strange, bleak landscape of God's seeming silence as we grapple with the kind of pain that could unravel us altogether.

Just after I began my battle with the OCD that would decimate my interior world and cripple my first foray into adulthood, I watched a beloved church go through a painful and bitter split. I watched my parents suffer the unjust, immature vitriol of two leaders who decided they had all the answers and anyone who didn't agree was no longer welcome. My sister began to have terrifying attacks of nocturnal asthma that my mom battled for hours in the midnight dark as my father worked away five nights a week. We lost our community. Within the year, we moved. And just before we did, I overheard a woman say to my mother, "Of course I feel sorry for you, but I can't really, because this is God's will, all of it, and he's using it for his glory."

Those words haunted me: ah, they do still. They severed what had been my last line of scrappy but radiant trust in God's love, in beauty, that held me sane throughout the dark episodes of my childhood. God's will? How was this an answer or comfort to the loss and confusion I felt? How was this any help to the world's suffering, to the school shootings and refugee crises and acts of terror that filled the headlines I began to obsessively follow? Before long, as you'll see, OCD came upon me in full, and my faith began to unravel along with everything else. How could I trust a god who chose and willed the agony of the world, the intimate destruction of my mind, the hurt of my parents, the bitterness of the church? The great, golden beauty I had known in my childhood seemed to me, then, an illusion, and God became one more broken thing lying in the darkness and yearning of my heart.

Until a feast thrown by the unlikeliest of friends helped me to remember the gentleness of a kindhearted Savior. Until a mighty story invaded my imagination and summoned me to answer for my hope. Until the touch and patience of those around me filled me with the knowledge of God's long, long suffering love. Until . . . I encountered beauty. Beauty in person and garden, art and song, story and starlight. A beauty that spoke of a reality beyond the touch of darkness. A beauty as pervasive again as that moment in my childhood. A beauty that summoned me to its own truth, that challenged me to journey beyond the flatlands of cynicism into the mountain ranges of a difficult and chosen hope.

Like Job, I was called into the wilderlands of mystery: the wild reality of a broken world where evil happens and God battles by laying down his life in love. Like Job, I was called out of the closed rooms of my neat expectations or pat theological assumptions, past my doubt and terror of God into the great battle and journey of living in a fallen world still invaded, pervaded, and beloved by the Creator who comes to draw all things back to health by his own unbearable breaking. Like Job too, I was summoned to an encounter with Beauty himself.

For just like Job, whose suffering was answered by the spectacle of God's vast creation (morning stars singing and oceans bound behind ancient doors and storehouses of snow and all the creatures great and small), I believe we are mightily and achingly addressed by beauty. I believe God cries out to us in our grief in the potent language of image and experience, answering our pain not with the explanations we may crave but with an experience of his goodness so tangible that we know hope, not as a proposition we speak but a burning in the blood, a tingling of the skin.

Beauty. That's the second story I truly believe we are all told in one way or another.

For beauty comes to us all in moments that unravel our cynical surety as our hearts seem to come apart at the touch of some odd slant of light on an evening walk. Or we hear the strained thread of some beloved old music that seems to break the spell of doubt. We read a novel, a story of someone who forgave or fought or hoped, and we feel something stir to life as precious, as fragile, as urgent as a newborn child within us. We are encountered by beauty, and suddenly the story of our grief seems to be the passing thing—that faint, ghostly illusion that one day will melt in the beams of a great, inexorable love.

My deep belief is that beauty has a story to tell, one that was meant by God to speak to us of his character and reality, meant to grip our failing hands with hope. We know God when we behold his beauty, when his goodness invades the secret rooms of our hearts. To believe the truth that beauty tells: this is our great struggle from the depths of our grief. To trust the hope it teaches us to hunger toward: this is our fierce battle. To craft the world it helps us to imagine: this is our creative, death-defying work. This book is the story of my battle to get my hands round beauty and hold to it through all the great and changing grief I have known. This is the song of hope I sing from out of the midst of my own darkness.

Beauty and brokenness told me two different stories about the world.

I believe that Beauty told true.

This is the story it told.

PART ONE

the truth beauty tells

1

This Is the Broken Place

A Shattered and Beautiful Mind

Sam saw a white star twinkle for a while. The beauty of it smote
his heart, as he looked up out of the forsaken land, and hope
returned to him. For like a shaft, clear and cold, the thought
pierced him that in the end the Shadow was only a small and
passing thing: there was light and high beauty for ever beyond
its reach.

J. R. R. Tolkien, *The Return of the King*

Alone, in the shadow of a pillar where my parents couldn't see
me, I stood barefoot on the redwood of our Colorado deck and
watched the first autumn storm break hard over the mountains.
The wind was up, wild, scampering down the foothills in front
of the cold front, bending the pines, pulling dark, smoky clouds
down the cliffs.

I watched and was afraid. And this was a sense so foreign to me that I was shocked, bereft of my own self and soul. For I had always loved storms. As a child, I had to be pulled back from the windows when the tornado warnings sounded, so mesmerized was I by the roiling of the sky and the oceanic clouds tinged green and black so that you felt you might glimpse an otherworldly horizon beneath them. Storms spoke to the hunger I bore even as a little person for some mighty beauty to break into my ordinary.

But that night, and in that storm, the only horizons I could see were the closed and darkened ones of my own mind. And the storm whose wind I could taste, whose strength pelted my skin, was a pale ghost compared to the wild weather within me, destroying my safety, wrecking the sure things I had known. "Mental illness" is such a tame, clinical term for what is actually an intimate disintegration of inward identity. A dark back door gets opened up inside a person's imagination, and the gnawing presence of something evil slips inside to scramble the world, distort every image, defile every loved thing.

I was seventeen years old, and everywhere I looked my mind showed me the people and places I loved caught up in graphic scenes of violence, perversion, and loss. The fleeting hints of this darkness I'd tasted in childhood were nothing to this new and terrifying invasion of my consciousness, a procession of defiling thoughts that never seemed to halt. I didn't yet have a name for my illness. I barely knew it was an illness, for I hadn't yet told a single other person what raged in me, but I knew I could no more escape it than I could escape my own body. For weeks, I had watched a horror film play in my head, and for a moment, hidden out there in the darkness, I could no longer resist the high, threatening voices I'd been fighting all day.

There will be no end to this.

There is no hope.

You can't bear this much longer.

What, then? I shivered convulsively, afraid to answer.

But then, a star shone. A single star in the navy sky breaking into the storm, and its shining was like a clear cry in my ear or a hand gripping my shoulder. Clean and hard, its brightness cut through shadow and mist, through the urgent, dangerous voices, and summoned me to attention. Out of the deep darkness of the gathering night, out of the violence of my gathered despair, I was called. I was gripped. I was held. The high, gentle starlight shone in its beauty upon my upturned face and I stood transfixed. For within that light I stood in an altered world. I tasted a loveliness so pure and ancient that for a moment I knew the darkness that roiled within me was a vain and passing thing. I knew that it could not touch what was essential within me, and beloved, for within that ancient light I also knew myself treasured by the Maker of all bright things, the keeper of storms, the weaver of stars. Within that starlight and in its command I stood, and where I stood, the world was remade and I was safe.

And then it passed. The voices screamed back. The wind tore at my face. And the images, the horrible images rushed in again. But the knowledge that had come to me in that moment of beauty was so real, so pervasively true, that for a moment, I was able to turn from the huge darkness brooding within me, from the shadows that beckoned me toward something I feared. I stepped into the light of the windows where my parents could see me and began, even as I opened the door, to summon the words I needed to tell them about the burden I could no longer carry alone . . .

"Beauty will save the world."[1]

Those words ring like a battle cry or a lover's declaration in the ear. They're from an old Dostoevsky novel, and I saw them first as the caption to a startling photograph just a few months into my full-blown wrestle with OCD. During the Bosnian conflict, when Bosnia was a moil of bombed-out buildings and broken lives, a classical musician dressed himself in a tuxedo and dragged his fine old cello into the ruins of the national library. Straddling debris, balanced between wreckage, he drew his bow and filled those aching ruins with music. He defied death with song. His music made a "truth" opposite to destruction. And glimpsing him, tasting the sweetness of that daring song for just a moment, those who heard him or saw the photograph afterward found themselves wondering if beauty really could somehow redeem a brutalized world.

Beauty, it saves us.

And I know this because it has saved me.

When my inmost world was a bombed-out room and I could see only abandonment and grief through the broken panes of my mind, Beauty came, "ever ancient, ever new,"[2] dragging a fierce loveliness into the ruins of my heart. He sat there amidst the shadow and stink of my mental illness, the broken stone of my shattered identity, my lost dreams, and began to make his music . . . of story and starlight, the touch of friends, the words of beloveds, image and song, sunset and wind. This Beautiful One broke into the darkness of my suffering, a God whose loveliness existed before the breaking of the world, whose goodness was a hand pulling me up, up, into the great, widened skies of hope where his love is at play for the healing of the cosmos.

God came into the very heart of my darkness—not in a show of power to cow my rebellious questions or as an argument to mollify my grief, but as a great and ancient Beauty whose goodness was laid in my fragile hands, whose purity was offered for my healing.

For almost twenty years now, I have lived in the daily company of mental illness, and the beauty of God is the only way I have kept my hold on sanity and a continuing belief that one day the world will be healed. Mine is a rarer form of OCD that means I am plagued by intrusive thoughts of violence, religious guilt, and sexual perversion. The intensity ebbs and flows, but when my illness is in its strength, I witness a world mottled with disaster, pocked with horror, all of it waiting to swallow up the people and things I love. How to explain?

I am seventeen, unable to look those I love in the face, for when I do I see perversion. I see the bodies and faces of those most precious to me caught up in acts of shocking sensuality I do not have the vocabulary to describe. I cannot stop or control what I see, and I see this everywhere I look. No person, whether stranger or beloved, is safe from my distorted vision. But I strive to feel no emotion, for when I feel grief or anger or frustration, an image comes to me of stabbing. Of my hands wreaking havoc upon those I love. I am undone with horror, bound in guilt. How can such dirtiness dwell in me, and is this truly my identity? Am I demon possessed or just despicable? I don't know. I simply do not know. For months I withdraw from my family and friends, terrified. And the secrets I don't know how to tell eat away the self I have always been and the life I have known until I no longer recognize the bleak world or the strange self I have become.

I am twenty-three and desperate to leave home but can't. Every time I try, I am plunged into a series of panic attacks so severe that the real and the imagined are blurred. No matter where I try to go, I am unable to sleep once night comes. My heart rate thunders as if I am running from an enemy, and my skin grows damp with dread as I witness countless devastating scenes. Image upon nightmarish image: the death of my mother, the grief of my father, the loss of my siblings, and more terribly, the sudden end of their love for me. Those stories of loss batter my imagination day and night. I become awkward with strangers, unable to engage with new surroundings because the inward barrage of those thoughts is like a wall around me even in daylight, and I only ever hold out just long enough to make it home.

I am thirty-two, a new mother with my tiny girl cradled in my arms. I walk with her by the window we have left open to ease the summer heat, and I see myself dropping her out of it, tripping and losing my grip upon her so that she flies into the summer blue air and crashes into the pavement a story below. I hear, oh God, I hear the breaking of her body, I see her sightless eyes. And the blood. And I stop, cowering back in the corner of my bedroom, my daughter clutched to me, unable for that moment to walk by the window. That image will come to me every time I pass an open window with a babe in arms for the next three years, shifting only to include the body of my tiny son.

I am myself, today, thirty-six, writing in my tiny study and half wondering if everyone I love will survive the morning. When my husband walks out the door, I wonder if he will ever return. When my children go for a walk with the babysitter, I begin to picture their funerals. I see a sharp corner on a sidewalk and witness the death of my toddler. When my mom or a friend hasn't called in a couple of days, I begin to wonder if they're sick, or depressed, or angry with me.

My faulty brain sees the possibility of death and disaster everywhere I look, and my broken mind tells me that the violence I see is the truest thing about the world. If I were to let it, this illness would overshadow the whole of my existence. It would tell me that life is only a bleak story, that we are made to suffer and our sorrow has no meaning. It would teach me to suspect every relationship, mistrust every promise. It would tell me that we are unprotected and unaided, alone in the shadows with everything we love at risk.

But this is the story darkness always tells.

This is what sin and sorrow and evil work in every one of us. My illness makes me witness to it in a visceral way, but none of us escape the shadow history that pain is always striving to thrust upon us. The disintegration of identity, the story-ending loss of hope: this is the darkness that threatens the inmost world of every single person who suffers. Pain tells us a story; that the loss and rejection, the anguish or abuse we have known defines our identity. That nothing is sacred and certainly nothing is safe. That we are trapped in a world whose violence we cannot escape. And in our breaking we begin to listen to the devastating words of the dark tale told by pain, the one that unravels any faith we ever bore in a God who heard our cries or answered our prayers. If this world is so dark, the story goes, then God must be angry. Or indifferent. Or, perhaps we've simply been abandoned.

Have I been tempted to believe that story?

Every day of my life. And in the beginning of my illness in particular, I nearly did.

But Beauty came, and Beauty saved me—from darkness, from unbelief, from destructive despair, from the bad answers that obscured his goodness, from the closed horizons of grief—and this is the story I have to tell.

You think you know what you're going to write when you start a book.

At least, I did when I began this one. I started writing during a family holiday to Denmark (my husband is half Danish). We stayed in a tiny cottage deep in the countryside, near the western coast, and every day my husband would whisk our little daughter down to the nearby shore to play while I sat at the kitchen table to write. I burned with the truth of what I wanted to create. I watched the red sun cast its rays across the bay, watched the wild swans dip and sway in the icy water, and I wrote feverishly. There was a dramatic edge to what I created as I sought to contrast the darkness I had known with the loveliness that invaded it. I was fresh from five years of theological study, and I wanted to write something that crashed into my reader's world like sunrise and music, like a fairy tale with all the satisfactions of a happy ending, all the questions answered and mysteries banished.

I came late to the study of theology. I reached my thirtieth birthday and felt profoundly lost in direction and identity after twelve years of OCD and its countless limitations upon my story. By way of coping, I found a one-year course in theology at good old Oxford and decided to go for an adventure. It was a half-baked, desperate plan, and how I managed to outlive the separation anxiety that usually crippled me is still a mystery. But three weeks into my studies, I discovered the term *theodicy*, a word describing the way we defend God's goodness and power in so evil and aching a world. I knew right then it was the subject I had been circling in the deep, defining questions of my faith throughout my adult life. I knew that this wrestling with God in the silence of pain had been my work since I was diagnosed with OCD, and I dug in my heels and began what would turn into two degrees and five long years of research.

Why do we suffer?

Why does God allow it?

Where is he when we are hurt?

The first books of theodicy I read offered arguments that felt like lawyers' briefs. I felt that God was their client, in need of legal protection against the anguished accusations of those in pain. The old words of my mother's friend, "I can't feel sorry for you because it must be God's will for you to suffer," echoed in my mind as I struggled through works on sovereignty and determinism, trying to understand theories in which God never loses control of any aspect of the world and yet cannot be blamed for its evil. The longer I studied, the more I began to resent the way that theological books so often meet pain with a list of arguments and doctrinal rationales. Your baby may have died, but everything works together for good. You may have a mental illness, but Paul had a thorn in his flesh and God left it there for greater purposes. You may have been abused, but didn't it make you compassionate? The more I read, the further God seemed from my pain. There were dark nights, in those early days, when I sat in the library and wondered if God could cause evil, if my pain was somehow necessary to the plot of his story.

But then, two great graces came to me.

First, a lesson. I came early one morning to the big lecture hall for a talk on doctrine. I remember the pound of the autumn rain on the panes, the way the overhead lights loomed bright against the grey world outside when a tall, friendly lecturer walked into the hall. He told one of the most ridiculous jokes I've ever heard, then launched into a talk on theodicy that made me sit up straighter, eyes brightening right along with my hope. This was theodicy by story, the real epic of a glorious and loving God who made the cosmos as the overflow of his glory. Once upon a time . . . God created, and it was good and existence was gift and grace, never intended for disorder or pain. But God, ever generous, made creatures in his very image and gave them the precious and radical gift of freedom. They were meant to use it as he did, for love and creation and joy. But they used his gift against him; they coveted God's power and used their own to rebel against him and each other and to disorder his beautiful gift of a world. So God sent his own Son to wage war by love, to conquer evil by self-sacrifice, to heal the world by the gift of himself. And the end of the tale, as with all the best old tales, was a wedding feast and a world renewed.

I sat at the end of the lecture feeling as if a door had been opened in a room where I'd been trapped. This story was one I could embrace as my own. This wasn't a disembodied idea but a narrative that translated my own pain to me in a way that dignified my suffering and drew me toward hope. It allowed me to understand my illness not as God's inexplicable will for me but as the evil he came to banish by his own presence. I carried the light of this knowledge with me as a secret joy that came to an even greater fullness when a tutor assigned me an essay on Job, that one great book of the Bible whose central theme is the exploration of God's presence in suffering. There, I found a theodicy I recognized, both in the story of my own life and in the ancient epic I'd heard in the lecture hall.

Job is a drama of questions, a story that echoes with honest anguish. Yet answers are never given in the listed, scientific way we think they ought to be in the modern world. At least, not by God, who was the only one who could answer Job truly. The terms of the story somehow forbid the kind of forensic revelations we so crave when we are hurt, and this was, oddly, a grace to me. For if one thing had become clear to me in my own suffering, it was that there is a mystery to theodicy, one we may not unravel this side of eternity. God does come—oh, he comes—but that doesn't mean the pain ends, yet. God doesn't tell Job why his children are dead and his house is in ruins. God doesn't explain to Job that he is part of a cosmic wager or that he hasn't actually done anything wrong. God doesn't offer explanation; but oh, he offers his own heartbreakingly beautiful self. God breaks into Job's darkness by actually allowing himself to be summoned by Job's cries for justice. He allows Job to question and grieve, to yearn and weep. But what he offers Job is not an explanation but an encounter. For Job is summoned to behold God's goodness in the staggering pageant of creation, one so mighty in its loveliness that at its end, Job considers himself answered.

Have you seen, says God, the birth of stars and the storehouse of the ocean? The moment when light was created and the sons of God shouted for joy? Have you seen springtime in its bright invasion of the mountains? Have you seen little babies all wrinkled and new with mothers alight in love; have you seen the bridegroom splendor of sunrise and the sinuous shimmer of dusk? Have you seen fields rippled with wheat and the mountains jeweled in snow?

God's answer to Job's suffering was just . . . beauty, and it was so thorough and true that Job was satisfied. It's not that his pain was zapped away in an instant, or that his loss was made small. God did not diminish what Job suffered, but there was God's aching request for Job to behold the kind of beauty that allowed him to live in the tension between God's power

37

and his own suffering, to trust that beauty, to let it speak to him of God's tenderness and power, to walk forward into the wild country of trust. I remember sitting in my college library at five in the morning when this realization came to me. The first threads of sunlight were glimmering in the trees at the far end of the garden out my window, and I was full of wonder. For this was a theodicy I recognized.

Here was the argument and grace of the starlight that kept me from an act of desperation when I was seventeen. Here was a theodicy that made sense of the strange moments of awed, wondering beauty I'd known throughout my dark years of OCD. I called them simply my *knowings*: instants of beauty that caught me off guard and left me flushed with wonder. The lilt of a Celtic song as I sat on my bed would suddenly stir and astonish me. In its notes I could hear the healing of the world. Or a line in a story that suddenly made me feel that the real saving of my mind and body would one day come. Or a blazing sunset, the curve of a mountain, the touch of my mother, the grace of a friend—they spoke hope into my long darkness in a language without words. They left me with no apologetic, no theological statement, but the real sense of God's goodness they imparted to me was the single greatest reason I still clung to my faith.

What if, in the bent and twisted darkness of our broken world, beauty is God's theodicy? What if God can speak in creation and song, story and vision the things words, in their frailty, cannot yet bear? What if God's hand reaches out to us clothed in beauty, and by grasping and trusting it, we may learn to walk through the darkness in hope?

This book came into being with that thought, and for the next four years, in between falling in love with my husband and having a baby and moving to another little town in England,

I read my way through stacks of theology. I immersed myself in works of literature and art, poetry and music whose beauty eased and answered my deepest suffering. I searched Scripture to see how God describes beauty, what role it plays in worship, how it invades the broken world, what it looks like as it comes to the poor and needy, aching for salvation. I gained confidence in my knowledge and began to form written debates against the kinds of theodicy that presented God as distant and uncaring in our pain. I signed up for my second degree and began to study the Enlightenment and how we came to value reason as more "true" than experience or revelation. I argued with philosophers (never a good idea). I wrote my dissertation on why Christian apologetics needed a whole new vision for theodicy.

And then I sat down to write this book.

I was bristling with ideas, bursting with explanations. Those first days in Denmark, what I set out to compose was a book to answer all the questions of suffering with beauty. The fragile self I'd once been, hands open before a stormy sky and in desperate need of healing, was in the past. I didn't want to be weak; I wanted to present my answer with as much power as those who seemed able to answer the sorrow of the world with a list of explanations. But what I was writing was an argument. An argument. And I didn't even realize I'd lost sight of the Beauty whose presence came as my healing until I found myself, again, immersed in grief.

The day we got home from Denmark we received a phone call. My husband's precious mother, a woman of warmth and faith like few I have ever met, a woman in her prime years with young grandchildren and decades of memories yet to make, had been told she had terminal cancer. Of course, at first, we were businesslike about it, thrust into the busyness of back-and-forth travel between our home in England and the Netherlands, where she lived. We thought there was time. We talked with the family about treatment options and extended life and that outer possibility that the cancer might respond and recede . . . for a season. We planned visits. I put the book aside. We operated, still, as if normalcy reigned.

And then, on a brief visit, my beautiful mother-in-law had a stroke, another blow in a series of shattering setbacks. And from that time forward, her condition deteriorated. We saw, firsthand, the dreadful ravages of disease in the human body: the aggressive cancer, the pain, the way disease steals, little by little, speech and ease, movement and consciousness. We watched from England, on tenterhooks, hoping for more time until the day we received another call. We needed to start driving if we wanted to say goodbye. By that evening, we stood at Susette's bedside, where she had clung to consciousness until we three, my husband and I and our toddler, Lilian, bent to receive her fierce, anguished, profoundly loving final embrace. In the early hours of the morning a day later, she passed away. From the day we found out her cancer would be terminal to the day she died, it was only four weeks.

My husband, an Anglican priest, led and preached at her funeral, and I witnessed the way that a life suffused by faith can transform even death. Susette's profound love for God and her family, her unshakable trust in God's goodness reached out even beyond her death to take our hands, to comfort her family as we sojourned together for a week after she passed. But when they lowered her body into the grave and I stood amongst her children, watched her husband hold their weeping youngest daughter, held the granddaughter who would never know her, and stood next to my grieved husband, her eldest son, I wept. Her loss was irrevocable.

And when we woke the next day, with all the tasks finished and the loving words spoken, a different grief settled in. The long, long silence of sorrow settled around us as we faced not the immediacy and drama of first loss but the years that must be reckoned anew in her absence, the countless moments in which her loss will sit like a new wound, opened afresh with each of the family events to which she will never come. We came home to England, and exhaustion, pervasive and deadening, caught up with us. We all caught colds. Our nights were disturbed. We moved slowly, navigating the wide grey silence that fills our inmost worlds when we grieve.

I sat again in my study sometimes, trying once more to pick up the threads of this book. The words I had written in Denmark sounded tinny to my ears, more like the lawyerish books I so despised. I found I couldn't write and couldn't pray. I knew again what it is to walk in darkness, to ask and hear no answer to the aching questions that so mercilessly attend the loss of what we love. Why did she have to die? Why did she have to suffer so deeply, be so destroyed physically? Why must such a luminous life cease from the earth when countless others cast shadows? As I sought answers to these questions, walking again in the shadowland of loss, I was reminded why I so vehemently oppose the answering of suffering by systems of theological assertion. There is no adequate explanation given in the cold voice of reason to answer our intimate experience of a loved one whose body disintegrates before our eyes.

But in that darkness, I discovered afresh why I so deeply believe that God does answer us: in the language of presence; in the gift of his own frail, human Son; in his world-making hands, clothed in countless tangible moments of beauty. He is here— not crashing in with light that makes our tear-sore eyes ache, or with demands that we believe in a list of assertions; he is here like a star whose tender light cannot be dimmed by a legion of darkness. He is here like the swell of new buds after winter. He is here like a lullaby sung in the night to a fretful child. He is here . . . like the stir and stretch of a child in the womb. My womb.

For as I sat again in those December days in the cold silence of suffering with my questions echoing in the dimness, my second child, a son, stirred in my belly. A child would be born to us, a son would be given to us; and his coming felt like a sign of renewal, a gift of God's beauty swelling to life just underneath my aching heart. The final days of my pregnancy took place during the hush of the Advent season, that time of spiritual twilight, when we remember that the Light of the world came, and comes, to those who yet . . . "dwell in darkness."

We kept a kind of vigil, watching for the coming of this child, waiting in the after-hush of his grandmother's death. Never in my life had I been so viscerally aware of the tension between the darkness in which we are tangled and caught and the hope that leads us forward out of it. Yet that tension, that strange middle place is where we wait for the kingdom to come. And in those days I knew again and again that these are the shadowlands where the light is growing; this is the quiet space into which Beauty speaks its truth.

But it's a fragile and often hidden beauty, the wisdom of God hidden from the worldly wise—and that's what I'd almost forgotten.

Fragile like a baby in the womb. The little son to come especially made me marvel; death at my back and birth before me, and in my own body, the rustles and thumps of tiny hands and feet, the dance of a little one whose hope-bringing life put me daily in mind of the baby born in Bethlehem two millennia before. In bearing that strange beauty, I became daily aware of the way hope yearned to be born in my heart. I knew a strange and unexpected joy in the words of Advent poems, at the echoed, aching beauty of Isaiah passages read in the half-light of the mornings, the plucky shimmer of Christmas tree lights, or the sweetness of my two little ones—one inside me, one outside, dancing circles round the Christmas tree—both of whose existence defied the power of death.

And I knew that God was coming in my grief, asking to enter the darkest room of my sadness not as a conqueror but as a child, knocking on the door of my heart with the tiny beauties of the ordinary, with healing in his hand.

I saw a star.

So what? Who hasn't?

I saw a star and its light was like something woven of hope and music, and the shimmer of it was a voice crying out to my spirit to keep hold, to take joy, and for a moment the whole of my suffering seemed unmade. The darkness became the false thing and the joy of that light, it was the truest thing I have ever known.

How can we believe what beauty speaks to us in the darkness of mental illness and cancer and abuse and death?

Because beauty calls to us with the voice of God.

We are answered not with argument or angry demands for obedience but with the presence of Immanuel, God here with us in the shadows. What beauty reveals is the intimacy of the divine in our grief. God gives us beauty, not as his argument

43

but as his offering—a gift that immerses us in something that allows us to touch hope, to taste healing, to tangibly encounter something opposite to disintegration and destruction. Where suffering has made God abstract and distant to us, where brokenness leaves us with unanswerable questions, beauty allows us to taste and see God's presence as he breaks into the circles of our inmost grief to remake the broken world.

Beauty offers us a theodicy of encounter. The beauty we find in the swaying fall of crimson, autumn leaves, in the taut notes of a Bach cello suite, in the poignancy of Caravaggio's *Incredulity of Saint Thomas* works upon us as evidence for something other than evil. The beauty we find in the touch of child or spouse, in the radiant face of a friend, in an act of kindness or justice, these allow us to taste and see goodness, alive and abroad in our broken world.

In that divine and present Beauty, the story of the world begins anew. Through beauty, we are called from the shadow-sight of pain into the opened horizon of hope. Story and song, storm and image, these help us to recognize a beauty beyond the touch of evil: something that lived before our pain, endures after it, and works to make us whole. In beauty, I believe, we encounter Christ, whose incarnate loveliness restored the broken world and is at play even now in creation—in art, music, and story, and in the presence of others as we are encountered by Christ in our neighbor, "lovely in eyes, and lovely in limbs not his."[3]

My son was born just after Christmas.

We named him Samuel, "God hears."

He was born at home, in our guest room. A candle glimmered on the windowsill, a playlist of old worship songs hummed as

I labored in warm water, and the room was close and dim as a summer evening when finally, he was born. There was a moment a little after the birth when we were both dried and wrapped on the bed and he was snuggled against my skin. My husband, Thomas, and the two midwives drew close, and the music we had on in the background, classical now, suddenly swelled (to Eric Whitacre's "The River Cam," I think) as we all stared at this tiny new person and he, quietly, stared back. One of the midwives suddenly laughed, startled by the wonder, saying, "This moment, it's, I don't know, it's so beautiful with this new little person and the music, it's just . . . perfect."

I think the word she might have wanted was *holy*.

Holy, because this tiny one, woven of love, is a sign of God's sweet life continuing in the world. Holy, because here we glimpse love in its sacred quiet, its unending renewal. Holy, because here in our hands amidst the sweat and messy room, the blood and fear, Love had arrived in the person of my little son, and it was beautiful. Beauty has come again amongst us: tangible, precious, healing our loss and promising that no precious thing ever is really lost after all. This is the hidden beauty that has transformed my life again and again in the seasons of my sorrow.

The writing of this book has taken place not only in the shadow cast by Susette's death but in the larger darkness of the COVID-19 pandemic. I've wrestled out the last pages amidst a twelve-week bout with pneumonia. I've watched the lives and weddings and hopes of precious friends get scuppered by lockdowns and quarantines. The world is full of grief, as it always is. But the goodness of God is coming, coming, coming.

His beauty is like a precious babe, grown great in the womb, reaching toward birth. He takes our grieved hands in the fragile, miraculous grip of newborn fingers. God's beauty is the kind that glimmered in a body that healed and cooked, whose hands stilled storms and welcomed children. He is the Beauty that rose from the very ashes of a violent death, who draws us onward into his light. Beauty that reaches out to us clothed in countless different hands and faces, woven with light, speckled with new leaves or bright stars, leading us forward into the healed world and the kingdom of heaven.

Beauty ever ancient, ever new—breaking into our darkness and making it light.

2

To Wrestle Is Righteous

The Third Gallery

Those who believe they believe in God, but without passion in the heart, without anguish of mind, without uncertainty, without doubt, and even at times without despair, believe only in the idea of God, and not in God himself.

Madeleine L'Engle, *Walking on Water:*
Reflections on Faith and Art

First, in the early days of OCD and the devastation it brought, I was Jacob. And oh, I wrestled hard with the Almighty.

I knew the old story well enough, that ancient account of God grappling hand to hand with a mortal. I'd found it bizarre at times, like a shard from a Greek myth shoved in among Scripture, the tale of a restless god who took it in his head to have a little fun in human form. Of course Jacob doesn't win.

Of course he becomes lame. *Strange people, those patriarchs*, I thought. But I hadn't walked long enough in the world to know how every human soul really does wrestle with God, how all of us shove up against him in the black dark of doubt. I didn't know how grief could make an endless night of my inmost thoughts, and how I could blame God for it with fierce, hot breath and yet ache for his touch at the same time, pleading for his light. I didn't know that wrestling was the only way, in this broken world, that I would ever get my hands around God's beauty in the midst of my pain.

Wrestle with God? I didn't know it was possible until I did.

One day late in the awful autumn of my seventeenth year, I hiked deep into the foothills of my Colorado home. The first searing months of illness lay behind me . . . the early days of silent, shocked pain as perverse and violent images became an almost minute-by-minute reality in my mind. Then the days of shame when I finally confessed what roiled within me. Then the weeks when my parents and I together tossed in the bewildering dark of mental illness, flailed for footing even as the wider world crumbled into uproar and my family planned a cross-country move.

In a strange confluence of events, the day my mind broke was the same one that terrorists flew planes into the World Trade Center towers in New York City. From the inward disintegration of a brain that twisted everything I saw into a graphic, disturbing image, I looked out at TV screens filled with flames and death, as desperate people jumped from high-rise buildings. Everywhere I looked, there was chaos. My sense of evil was of something riotous and powerful, roaming the world, unstopped and irresistible. As my parents sought pastors (one told me I was demon oppressed) and psychiatrists (one told me

I needed prescription drugs immediately, but she couldn't fit me in for another six months) and tried to keep us from cratering, I looked wildly about for some glimpse of the God I had spent my whole life believing was full of power and goodness.

But he seemed to have disappeared, and one day when the anguish of it was more than I could contain, I walked out the door and made for the mountains. I walked as fast as I could until I reached the shadows of a pine glade with tree-tangled light and tumbled, broken stones like sleepy giants in the gloom. In better moments, I had imagined this place a chapel. That day, it was my dungeon, my secret place in which none but God would hear my sorrow.

None but God and the boy who died.

The glade had always felt sacred, hushed with the breath of old pines, but death had also made it holy. A teenage boy had taken his life there, and the clearing was marked at its center by a memorial built by his brother, a jagged red pile of mountain stones with a G.I. Joe toy fixed to a concrete plaque. The loneliness of that bent little figure set a lump in my throat. I sat down next to the pile of stones, settled into the dirt, felt the cold of the earth seep into my skin. I fingered the G.I. Joe and kept vigil with the boy who fought, and somehow lost, there in the lonely forest.

God, I breathed. *God*, I hissed. *God*, I wept.

Sometimes I envy people who had a conversion, a "come to Jesus" experience. "Everything is different now," they say, and it seems that their image of what it means to be saved is clearer than mine, a point of transformation to which they can return in times of suffering. For me, God has always been around. First child of missionaries, I prayed a prim little salvation prayer in my frilled nightgown at five years old, and I can still remember

49

meaning it with all my heart. I always have. And while I am keenly aware as the years progress that a home rich in faith is a rare gift, it also means that I know God in the workaday way that I know my parents; he is behind their high standards for my behavior, behind the rhythm of prayer I have known since babyhood, the one we thank, the one we implore. He is like my grandfather, the one I knew from a distance: benevolent, kind, a bit stern.

And absent. Sitting in the dirt that day, a seventeen-year-old girl at her first moment of crisis, I felt that I had never known God at all. All I had were questions. The piled doubt of months was a crushing weight on my heart, and I realized that being good for a distant deity no longer sufficed. The hands of my soul reached out into the formless dark of my questions, the ones I had never asked. I flailed in the dim, black void in which each human exists in a loneliness they only begin to taste in pain. I sat there and sobbed, and if I prayed, it was one long shout of rage and bewilderment, so bitter I wondered if I'd ever hear from God again.

But amidst my outrage, God came.

How can I describe this? What can I say to evoke what it is to find God with you at the heart of your darkness except to say that in the middle of a teenager's nervous breakdown in a pine forest, he was there. He was there: a presence and form just beyond my sight, keeping vigil with me in the shadows. When I railed and wept, I was not speaking into a void, I was addressing a Person.

And suddenly I was Jacob, in the wilderness, wrestling with God for my life.

In the half-light of those foothills, I struck God first with my pain, because it shocked me. Before OCD I knew people suffered and dark things happened beyond the confines of my fairly innocent life. But evil was a force I neither knew nor chose, yet God had allowed evil to take up residence in the inmost rooms of my being. Was this his doing? I was Eve as well as Jacob—Eve when the world was stripped of beauty, when the first stab of grief rent the air and the ancient, bewildered groans of humanity began. *Why? Where is God?*

I wrestled next with myself. I didn't mean to. I wanted only to grapple with God, but locked in his arms, my eyes inexorably turned to my angry heart. Dry as the bottom of the ocean drained of all its water, the desert of my life stretched around me. Was a bit of it my own making? It could be. In that hot moment, I knew that I had a trickster soul like Jacob's, a heart that thought it could outrun pain. I thought I deserved to be blessed, that the Christian pedigree of my family would protect me. I knew that OCD wasn't my fault, but the anger that welled in me like molten fire, the hostility toward any word of comfort to turn me from my despair, this belonged to me. Frailty was in my very bones, and in God's hands I knew it as never before.

Finally, I wrestled with God's supposed goodness. For fallen though I was, my existence was his fault, and if he really was the mighty and good being I had trusted him to be, then my pain was too. The pain of the whole world belonged to none but him, and I struck him with that as hard as I dared. How dare he call himself good while darkness ravaged his beloved? How dare he call himself strong when evil stole our innocence? How dare he name himself Savior if so much could still be wrenched from us? I stretched and strained in the darkness of questions. I wanted to escape this God or defeat him, to name him weak or blame him and leave.

But even as I struck him with my accusations, I became aware of my anguished desire for his love. He was the cause of my grief, the opponent, and the peace I craved all in one enigmatic, awful Beloved. I could no more walk away from his existence than I could walk away from my own desire for breath. Every question I bore, every strike was to and for him—no part of my story explained apart from his troublesome existence. He was my opponent and my prize, my enemy and the lover I yearned for with all of my being, and he held me even as I flailed against him.

When my anger was spent, I leaned back against the red rocks, if not lame like Jacob, then exhausted. The air was musty, my face wet, my sight blurred. But a gleam of twilight struck something just beyond my fingertips and my breath caught. A small host of treasure had joined the G.I. Joe since my last visit. The little soldier bumped shoulders with plastic angels and animals, tin crosses, and old toys. Friends and strangers had left their tokens in the blind hope that the soul of a brokenhearted boy could be healed beyond death.

I fingered the tiny G.I. Joe as it clung tenaciously to its rock, a symbol of such defiant love left by a grieved brother. One boy lost his battle there in the forest, but the other took up the fight in his honor, and, in the fierce pain of that memorial, I glimpsed the kind of beauty that is not so much the vision of something good as a defiance of the evil that is all you can see at the moment. There was holy tenacity in that little mound of toys, the sign of a few souls clinging hard to the possibility of some great goodness beyond the touch of darkness, a Beauty so radically opposite to death that it might even rescue those lost in the valley of the shadow of death itself.

And this was the Beauty who came to wrestle with me.

I understood that, abruptly. Into the void of my spent anguish, into the black of my exhausted need, came the gentle goodness of God, like fireside warmth into a cold room. He rested there with me in the twilight, a strange presence who did not explain himself or rebuke my anger but gave himself into my anguished hands and made of my wrestling a holy thing. He broke into the shadows obscuring his face and gripped me with the hands of a searing and precious hope. He wrestled with me and made my struggle a reaching toward something beyond my loss, something entirely other to the darkness. To grip this enigmatic God with all my fear and doubt was not, I realized in that moment, the end of my faith, but perhaps . . . its beginning.

I lifted my eyes to where the sky was fading into an opalescent blue behind the sword points of the pines. That sky, under which a whole world wept and burned. Could there be a Beauty vast enough to cradle and transform the history of our shattered darkness? I saw the huge concavity of the darkling sky, where daylight clung to the last clouds in a few vivid threads of gold. *Hold fast.* The words whispered in me, and I understood that nothing was asked of me in that season of pain but the will to hope that the Beauty I so desired could be true. I thought, perhaps, I could.

This world is the broken place and we are broken within it.

This is the hard and devastating word I learned through my illness, the word that comes to each of us born into terrifying and lovely existence. In a world wrecked by sin, our pain is the crucible in which we will work out our faith. No human story is exempt from grief. There is no faith without the wild ache of impossible questions. To wrestle with God—to grip him like Jacob with hungering, angry hands—is the work of every person born into a fallen world. This is what it means to be human and follow God in a world at war, wrenched away from the Beautiful One who crafted its being.

But the way we wrestle will shape the whole of our story, and Beauty tells us what we are wrestling for.

I never knew, until that mountain evening, that struggle was intimately part of devotion. I thought that wrestling with God meant I was doing something mightily wrong. Doubt and terror, fear and anguish? Surely these are the marks of sin? I thought that if my belief was strong enough, I would march forward like a soldier into maturity. I thought that's what it meant to walk by faith, not the drunken, battered stumble of a grieved soul just stubborn enough to grasp God by the fingernails for one more day.

I was shocked by my suffering, because I hadn't reckoned with the real fallenness of the world, and I wonder if my shock is a common one in the modern Christian world. I think we God lovers are often bewildered by personal disaster, troubled by the reality that being saved doesn't mean we'll never suffer. We haven't really come to terms with the fact that the first part of our story is a tragedy. It doesn't jive with the missional excitement of God's "good news," with our marketer's promise of blessing to those who accept God's love. It doesn't fit the progressive narratives of science and technology that so often get tangled up in our spirituality. It doesn't work within our arithmetical idea of obedience: if I'm good, God will bless me. We forget what it means for the world to be fallen and for us to be profoundly frail, and when suffering comes upon us—and oh, it does, to godly souls and innocent children, the evil and the good alike—we are outraged and bewildered. We stand in danger of abandoning the very faith whose power is based on divine love overcoming death, because we didn't think we really had to die in the first place.

The gospel is good news: oh yes, it is the single radiant fact that can heal the world. But it's a truth invading the rocky and troubled soil of the fallen cosmos. If we have not grasped that God's goodness comes to us *in* the darkness, not just that of the general world but of our shattered and faulty selves, that he is our comfort *when* we walk through the valley of the shadow of death—not just a death outside us in the headlines but the one we taste as intimate terror—we have not understood what it means to follow and love the crucified Christ, the suffering servant, the wounded God whose very life was required for the healing of the devastated world.

But the hard word of our brokenness is also the word that sets us free and teaches us to fight. Like King Lear in Shakespeare's great tragedy, blinded and stripped of all he loved, we learn to "speak what we feel, not what we ought to say." What we feel is grief, and in the hands of God, it becomes a mighty and holy thing. We were not created for disaster nor formed for destruction, and to lament our pain is to honor the beauty God intended and yearn toward its restoration.

For yearning is the heart of what it means to wrestle.

"The only possible defence for God against the charge of making a world riddled with suffering and violence is that He didn't," writes my Oxford tutor, Michael Lloyd.[1] Our origin is love, and we were intended for blessing, not destruction. The point of our struggle is not to gain some sort of spiritual grit or prove our endurance. We are not asked to become grim warriors in the face of pain; we are asked to be children who will not rest until they know themselves cradled in the arms of the Father who begot them for joy. The point of our wrestling is that God himself has arrived in the midst of our sorrow, a gracious Savior who gives himself into our desperate hands and teaches us what it means to grip the reality of our salvation, our restoration to glory. In God's hands, we wrestle *toward* hope, we fight our way *onward* to fresh belief.

The mystery of suffering may be great, but God's location within our suffering isn't. He is here, holding us as we suffer a broken world, tugging us forward toward the healing and surety we can find only in his gracious hands.

The real risk to faith is *not* to wrestle, and I know this because, for a while, I stopped. And I stopped because of what people told me about God.

In the months that followed my mountain breakdown, I began to ask hard questions surrounding my illness. Shy, reluctant, I took them every now and then to a pastor or mentor. But the answers often bewildered me. "God's will is mysterious, but it's perfect and everything that happens is in his control," said one. "You need to figure out what he's trying to teach you." (Well, Lord, I find R-rated mental images rather confusing, but tell me, what should I take from this?) One pastor I read wrote an article on a public disaster and said we should be thankful for grace because the people who perished only suffered the death we all deserve. "God will use this," said the very few I trusted with my story. "You need to figure out what you're supposed to learn."

But what did that mean? That God would demean himself to the level of horror to get me to do his will? Was I so difficult that OCD was necessary to humble and shape me? The answers I was given were so sure, as if suffering were a crossword puzzle I simply had to work out, set for me by a stern, immortal teacher. But I was, it seemed, a failure as a student, for I couldn't see the good in the evil of what transpired in my mind.

I began to suspect the God I had just begun to hold, and this instigated a confusion that would last many years, fueled often by answers that tried to wrap up pain in a containable package. Shaped by those answers, I began to believe that the darkness around me was of God's making. I began to think I saw a God who used suffering as a way of making people behave. God as Creator, yes; God as merciful on the vast scale of history; but God as distant in the agonies his plans made in the hearts of women and children and . . . girls like me. I stepped back from his hands because he scared me. I stopped reading Scripture because my dread blinded me to God's mercy. I still believed in him—the long habit of faith, the love of my parents, moments of beauty, they tethered me to belief—but I struggled to hope or pray.

I wrestled, but it wasn't with God: it was with the ideas that obscured him.

And God was enveloped in the shadow of my fear: a great hulk of menacing divinity that stared out at me from my imagination, a presence I did not want to face because the eyes would be angry, the mouth hard against me and my frailty. My mind was already filled with images that terrified me; I couldn't bear this one too, so I turned my face away from my Maker. For how can you wrestle toward hope if you think God is the one who has taken it?

Sometimes I wonder if it's our fear of sorrow that drives us to answer the deepest suffering around us in words that God himself never used. We are afraid to admit the depth of our brokenness, to sit with our tears and let them speak to us of our fragility and our need and our eternal hunger. We would rather God be neatly culpable for the evil that comes upon us, would rather believe that cancer and infant death and abuse and tornadoes are explainable as necessary to the overarching story of the world, than face the kind of ancient, true drama in which God himself weeps at the sight of what he has made, now defiled and destroyed. We are afraid to sit in the wild presence of sorrow, allowing it to whisper to us of a Savior who mourned the death of his friend and wept on the night he was sent to death himself.

But if we do not weep, how can we allow ourselves to be saved and sated by the God who called himself the Suffering Servant? How can we receive the grace of the Savior who collects each tear we cry in his world-making hands?

It took an art museum and a gorgeous old church to get me wrestling with God once more.

Somewhere within those years of my doubt, I went on a journey with my mother back to the country of Poland, where she had lived as a missionary in her single days. One raw, brisk morning, after hours of nostalgic wandering, we slipped off the cold streets to shelter in an art museum. I love art museums. I love most to visit them in a country whose history I don't know well, because a people's art tells a story, and not just the tale of this war or that kingdom. Castles or knights, songs or families, the masterpieces a people create are the record of what they hope to remember right down the steps of the fast-falling years.

The story that day promised joy.

Fluid and fragile, the light of early spring shimmered from windows high in the white walls, pulsing with the energy of wind and sunlight. The quality of the air was rich with the same quiet that comes with prayer, but the energy beneath it was like laughter, and the merriment came from the paintings and portraits, the massive images filling the broad walls.

You could almost hear the laughter between those portraits—giant images of handsome, doughty men in military splendor, pictures of women with arch smiles and rich dresses, bold in their beauty and glance toward the viewer. Landscapes stretched between them, verdant fields and orchards thick with ripened fruit and houses settled deeply into the earth. I remember the children best, the paintings of little ones, in their gauzy dresses and billowy pinafores, tucked in beside their mothers or in the high grass of a meadow or under the roses in a garden. I walked through the room, unable to rest for long at any one painting, because each seemed to call to the other. The room was alive with the leap of painted glances, the echoes of timeless laughter.

I reached the end of the hall and stepped into a small court-yard. Another door opened before me. Curious, I stepped through a much lower arch into the second, narrower gallery.

I stopped. To this moment of writing, I can taste the horror, heavy and sour on my tongue and soul, that met me at sight of the first painting. Gaunt, bent bodies scattered broken over dirty snow, dull sky and hard walls hemming them in. I stared. Forgot to breathe. Began to shiver as if some door had let in a cold, cold wind. In a sort of mental shock, I lurched to the next painting. A picture in all blue tones of a boy with a whitened face and absent air, black hair over eyes that did not even register fear from the guns pointed hard at his chest, the white body crumpled at his feet. I moved on. This gallery was long and low, the hall snaking ahead of me in shadow. The pictures loomed large on the walls in a silence that froze me still and trapped my feet until horror forced me on. The lines in each were stark, gashes of color sketching scenes of war and death in a mixture of strokes so swift it seemed the artist could not look long on his subject, wanting to escape the scene he crafted even as his own hand made it immortal. I felt the same: unable to look away but longing for escape as I followed the gallery round. When the exit door yawned before me, I nearly ran for it.

In the little courtyard once again, crushed between the ghosts of what felt like two different worlds, I sat down. My mind could not reconcile those vastly divergent stories, for both told the tale of the same people. Two galleries. Two stories. The first the tale of a golden age when the people inhabiting modern-day Poland had rivaled other kingdoms of Europe in splendor; the second, the tale of the ravaging loss that came with WWII. One of a beauty so exultant it seemed indestructible. The other the tale of its breaking, a shattering so complete it seemed that the beauty never was and never could come again.

What, I wondered, breathless, came after? When you have known such beauty, and felt such horror, what story do you tell when both are done? What third gallery was, even now, in the making, and what would its makers choose to tell with such opposing histories behind them?

What story would I choose to tell?

Caught between those two vivid histories, I abruptly recognized myself, and as I did, I knew the presence of my Maker sitting there with me. I didn't expect him, and the quiet of that tiny antechamber was heavy upon me, heavy between us. He came again, as he did on the mountain, and my heart burned as I understood that those galleries embodied the recent history of my soul. Beauty and darkness. Grief and grace. Despair and laughter. I too had opposing galleries in my heart.

A first gallery, rich with the in-breaking beauty of God, of starlit moments and love that took my aching hands and taught me to hope for healing. A gallery filled with the grace of a wrestling God who gave himself to me and drew me onward into a hope I couldn't yet imagine. But a second gallery, stocked by pain and worked by fear, the landscapes of my worst thoughts and lost dreams, the portraits of a God with angry eyes, or hardened hands, or just an old man both angry and distant. And I was standing with my foot stuck in the gallery of darkness.

I had believed the horror rather than wrestling with God for the beauty I had known and the beauty that lurked, somewhere beyond the shadows.

Sitting there I understood that one of the great battles fought in this battered and precious earth is the one waged by the human heart to reimagine God as good when pain and fear have hidden his face. Despair is the long and subtle work of evil. Satan triumphs within our suffering, not just in the bringing of pain but by wrecking God's radiant image within our imagination. And his final work is that gallery in our inmost soul in which God's image grows as a horror. I knew, in that moment, that God had been lost to me when I believed false things about him.

I looked up and saw a third door in the anteroom, opened just a crack with a line of spring sky visible through it. Through the slim opening came a sly, cool wind that danced into the still air of that place. The wind gusted harder, shoving the door a little farther open, and light spilled in, a river-like brilliance that set the air shimmering. The glory drew my eyes. I wanted to walk out the door into the freshened world beyond my bewilderment. And in that moment, I understood that in a way, that's what I was invited to do.

There was a third gallery waiting for me. A hall where God was at work creating something I couldn't yet imagine. A gallery composed not of the beauty I had lost or the pain I had suffered, but of both those things caught up in a new artistry wrought in me by the God who called me to wrestle with my pain, to reach for him with hope. A gallery where weeping could weave with mystery and faith to create an inner space of such beauty that it could defy the story told by evil within the world.

But how? How could I find or create or receive that beauty into myself?

Redemption was a word I couldn't quite comprehend at that point. Having heard it all my life, I associated it with what happened to sin-blackened hearts, but I wasn't sure what it meant for good little God-fighting girls like me. I hadn't yet understood it as the goodness of God invading my most intimate moments of depression, taking the shards of my broken self and setting about the work of new and mended creation. I still thought redemption was one big event that God did, not the whole of my daily story transformed by his generous life.

But one thing I knew. I could not find it unless I took God's hands in mine once more. I could almost hear the invitation in the mischievous wind invading that space: *Will you wrestle?* As wry and lively as if it were an invitation to dance. And in a way it was, for in that place I began to understand that wrestling might not be the fight against God I had thought it, but a lover's tangled whirl into a new world. I offered God my hand, though I wasn't yet sure what would happen.

A month later I stood in an Anglican church in Nashville. Having read great reams of Madeleine L'Engle, Tolkien, and C. S. Lewis in my months of doubt, I woke one day to the fact that they all were liturgical worshipers. Whatever they had, I wanted a taste, so I dragged my family down to the best known of the Anglican churches in Nashville (where we had recently moved), a honey-bricked, homey church with the affectionate name "St. B's."

The beauty of it caught me first: the gem-toned windows scattering ruby and sapphire and emerald light over my face. The lit candles, the cross, square and center, almost a countenance facing me as I walked in. And the story. Never in all my churchgoing years had I been so aware of enacting a narrative in the Scriptures read, the creeds affirmed, the prayers spoken in tandem with countless thousands around the world. But my moment of epiphany came when I rose to receive the Eucharist before an altar. When I bowed under that cross, when my knees nudged the carpet and a stocky priest with a red beard very kindly pressed the bread into my hands and whispered, "This is Christ's body, broken for you," the world, for one great remaking moment, stood still.

His body . . . broken.

Broken like the beautiful world he made and the hearts of those made in his image. Crushed like my own hope and mind. Shattered like the countless thousands gripped by war. God's body: broken in and with the world that was meant to be his pure, wondrous gift. But at the cross, broken as gift. We humans wrestle with God, but God wrestles with death itself. He takes every evil act and scream of pain into the great strength of his heart, and instead of crushing it all and us with it, allows his own priceless self to be crushed. He wrestles, and writhes, and dies—the one human who can win the fight against evil—and in his holy defeat, we finally overcome. God does not stand aside from our suffering, directing it to his ends. He enters it, and by the sacrifice of himself transforms it into the space where we may know his deepest love. I held that bread and understood that the body of Christ is the last broken thing, the one that in a mystery, draws every broken heart into a love so mighty that death itself turns backward within us to life.

I ate, then rose and shuffled back to my pew, walking the aisle back to my seat, shy as always, but in that moment so brimful of my new understanding that I dared to keep my eyes up as I walked. My gaze was captured by the row of stained-glass windows on my left-hand side. A gallery, it seemed, of living light, reflected in the forms of diamond-eyed saints and ruby-hearted martyrs. Down the chapel they marched, a line of shimmering portraits amidst whose splendor I walked.

And then an older woman caught my eye on the right, with a glint in her glance as bright as the diamonds in the stained-glass saints. I glanced back shyly and smiled. My gaze turned more thoroughly beyond myself than it had in many months as I beheld the odd assortment of humanity in the church that day: old and young, solemn or half-merry in their seats, every heart bearing both the grief and beauty of the human life that is a broken gift remade by a broken God. Every one of us had knelt, every one of us in need of that healing bread. I felt a great camaraderie with the host around me. The sanctuary was hushed but it was charged with the energy of the hope given at the altar. Each person I passed, each saint in the stained-glass windows, was a living image of redemption.

And abruptly, I knew that I was standing within the third gallery I so longed to find, right in that moment of shared sacrament and sight. For we who took God's body and life into ourselves were the great new works of art that make up the third gallery of the world. That space was crammed with the living images of redemption. The third gallery was here, and the portraits were the living ones of the saints who are new creations of their God. I knew myself surrounded by living masterpieces, by our forebears in the windows and my comrades in their pews. I knew that every one of us was a living picture of the Love who has come among us, our lives his portraits, painted in the vivid hues of redemption.

3

Beauty Is Truth

Love Sets Us a Feast

> Earth's crammed with heaven,
> And every common bush afire with God:
> But only he who sees, takes off his shoes;
> The rest sit round it, and pluck blackberries,
> And daub their natural faces unaware
> More and more, from the first similitude.
>
> Elizabeth Barrett Browning,
> *Aurora Leigh*

I didn't expect to step into the garden of Eden when I walked out the door.

I didn't expect anything at all that day, curled up as I'd been in a cramped room with ceilings on which I bumped my head and thoughts that left my faith no room to stand up straight. It was my total lack of expectation, a sense that everything beautiful had gone beyond my touch, that made the beauty of the garden so startling. I walked out the door of the old student house into late, honeyed light in an English garden and abruptly felt like Eve walking into a newborn world.

I felt as if blood was returning to my senses, as if they'd been numbed and I hadn't even known. A buzz of voices swelled happily round me as I walked farther into the light. I stood in the shadow of the shabby but gracious old English house where I was living while I worked for the summer as an intern at a nearby church. I'd lived in that house for six weeks, yet I felt as if I were truly seeing the garden for the first time, and it was like the secret garden I'd read about in the old favorite story of my childhood. Ivy clothed the weathered red brick of the house, apple trees grew haphazardly around the green lawn, and the old garden beds were a riot of flowers—lavender and climbing roses and towering lupines.

A party awaited, the reason I'd come to begin with, for one of my housemates was moving and throwing himself a going-away picnic. But I hadn't expected such a feast. Three wooden tables were set against the stone wall at back of the garden with huge, cracked old bowls crammed with stemmed straw-berries or golden melon and patterned with scenes in china blue. There were piles of cheese, more than I had ever seen in one place outside a store: brie melting gently, Wensleydale with its starring of fruit, Stilton and cheddars with crackers and olives lumped around them. The last table almost toppled with innumerable bottles of wine, the dark glass glinting under the sun.

The light was thick like honey, low in the sky so that the shadows grew long under the trees and tangled their gentle darkness with the gold. I felt it around me as the gentlest of warmth, easing my tired mind, brightening my eyes, and out of that brightness, my friend came to greet me.

"Sarah, you came! I am so glad," he said, and two kisses were quickly set, one on each cheek in European style, as my hands were gripped and pressed. "There's so much to eat, get a plate and join us."

I started after him, but halted, just an instant, as the strange feeling of something like relief flooded into my heart. Until that moment, I hadn't realized that I was starving. That the body and soul of me, however nourished in the ordinary ways, were almost wild with yearning for touch and laughter, for people to see me and want my company, for beauty I could hold in my hand and taste in my mouth. I had spent long weeks enduring a hunger for color and touch and music I did not address because I did not think it was important. Yet it was that very unmet ache whose yearning led me to the lonely Saturday I had just spent in a high, shadowed room in an old house, thinking that faith was a dim thing and God an idea I could no longer desire.

But the touch of my host's hands drew me out of darkness and into the light of human affection. The taste of strawberries and sparkling wine and brie startled me into a joy I had forgotten. The rich beauty of God's summer world, with that sly, merry light, found me in the garden—and in the startling joy of it, I reached for God's hand. Amidst the feast whose loveliness was melting my loneliness, I began to wonder if the hunger that had become a ravening void at the center of myself led not to death, but joy. . . .

We're born hungry.

We humans, thrust into a world meant to speak to us of our Maker yet somehow echoing with his absence, bear a precious and divine hunger from birth. It's God we want, and the kind of hunger we bear is like passion and tenderness; we want to eat and touch God, drink and breathe him. We want to hold him close and breathe in his loveliness like we would a small child or a beloved spouse. Our suffering and grief only make this worse, for this precious God in all his beauty is the one who made us, the only one who can unmake our pain and restore our joy.

But what does it mean to know the love of God?

How does one feast upon God's goodness in the desolate field that is the human heart after grief?

Sorrow and hope, grief and grace in their tangle throughout my twenties made me ravenously hungry to know God's love in a tangible way. I wanted to grip him, curl myself into his arms, feel the real warmth of his breath. I knew that for some, the brave and luminous people I'd known and read about, faith in God could mean palpable joy and peace you could take in your hand like an apple whose firm succulence could cool your hunger. But how does one have the kind of faith to take the apple in hand? What does it really mean to "taste and see" that God is good amidst a fallen world?

Beauty tried hard to teach me.

For years, in the strange, swift moments I called *knowings*, I tasted something I thought, with shock and joy, could be called the goodness of God; I *knew* something true about his nature. The swell of a choral piece as I sat on my bed in loneliness could suddenly stir and astonish me. In its beauty I could hear the healing of the world.

Or a sunset over a Tennessee field after another of my solitary, restless walks when I felt myself sliding toward depression and was stopped by the sight of the sky, washed in a cascade of colors. Standing there, for just an instant, I was whole and unafraid and so loved my skin broke out in goose bumps.

Or just a bowl of apples sitting in a pool of sunlight on an old wooden table. The gleam and curve of their shape, the burnished color, the way they sat there promising apple pies and cider and laughter; it all seemed so pervasively good I couldn't believe that apples were ever created for sorrow.

Ah, beauty. In a dappled sky, or a folk song, the peak of a mountain, the touch of a friend: beauty set me a feast amidst my sorrow, instants of profound joy that sated my hungry heart. I felt Love at play in and through them, reaching out to nourish that deep hunger for God at the core of my being. "All that exists is God's gift to man and exists . . . to make man's life communion with God, it is divine love made food,"[1] and in my *knowings* I tasted this truth.

But over and over I dismissed beauty as having any real bearing on my spiritual hunger or the larger story of my faith. Those instances of *knowing* seemed such small, ordinary things— powerful yet fleeting. And I had been trained by the culture around me, even that of my church, to dismiss such trivialities as imagination or emotion; art or music or the joy I felt in nature were frivolous things, pleasant in their way but incapable of bearing Truth (with a capital *T*). I was so deeply formed by the age in which I lived that I didn't yet understand that I could trust what a fallen leaf or an autumn feast, a lilting song or the coming of spring was speaking to me as true. I didn't see that these small glories had been offered to me as communion with my Maker.

"O taste and see that the LORD is good" (Ps. 34:8 NASB). The last meaning we usually give this verse is a literal one, and it was the last that occurred to me despite the fact that my moments of beauty were the only place I had ever come close to knowing God's reality. We live in an age (a "secular age" says Charles Taylor in his book of the same name) where we have been told for centuries that what you see is what you get. We don't even realize the extent to which our view of God and ourselves is shaped by materialism, what Wendell Berry in the subtitle of his book *Life Is a Miracle* calls a "modern superstition" because it's a belief that the touchable world of science and matter is all there really is.

Augustine called the created world a book written not with ink but the stuff of the cosmos, with everything in it reflecting and revealing the mind of its Creator. For ancient believers, the world *meant*: storm and song, starlight and season—these came straight from God's imagination, and they told us something vital about his character and heart. But we moderns dismiss this as fancy and view the world with disenchanted eyes as a collection of atoms and dust—something to measure but not something that means. We struggle to see the stuff of earth, the food we eat, the homes we craft, or even the love we make as sacred, caught up in redemption and capable of offering us the continuing goodness of God.

"Knowing" now means just facts, and too often, we've thought those facts could capture God. But can we really know the soul and its hungers in the same way we measure the temperature? Can the heart and its yearning be observed under a microscope? May God, in the mystery of his mercy transforming our pain, be known by formula? Can we sate our sorrow by a system?

For a little while, I thought so.

For a little while, I thought that maybe I could know God's love and taste his goodness if I had all the right facts about him. I'm not sure where I came by this assumption, but it's one I see echoed in countless lives around me. We meet suffering and doubt with a brisk directive to study. I wonder if our way of knowing God, our way of giving him to others has been so formed by the ideas of science that we think we can offer God like a presentation and find him like the solution to a science experiment. I thought that if I could gather enough theological information to understand the complex workings of suffering and goodness and God's will, I could get him in hand like that apple. Faith, I thought, must be a kind of mathematics I could learn where all the sums would add up right. And if I could solve the puzzle, perhaps the desperate ache I bore to know God's love, to taste his presence, would finally be eased.

————————

So I went to England in search of explanations.

It seemed a likely place to find them since I'd been enamored of C. S. Lewis and Oxford academics since my teens. I was in my midtwenties, hungry for fellowship and answers, when I found a summer internship at a church hosting a conference on systematic theology. Systematic! This was what I craved, and my need to know, far more than any amount of shame or effort had yet done, pushed me to defy my OCD and brave the looming dark of separation anxiety and jet-lagged panic attacks that would probably last most of my two-month stay. I applied. I was accepted. I packed my bags for England and readied myself for answers.

The internship was, of course, a thing of long hours, many errands, and endless menial tasks. The church where I worked was in the city center, and I rose early each morning to snatch some breakfast and try for some prayer in the little garret room at top of the huge old house where I lived. Then I walked to work through the back gardens of the colleges whose grounds crossed the river. At first, I met those cool, early mornings with a sense of possibility. Mist hovered over the quiet river, the creamy stone of the college buildings with their diamond-paned windows loomed through the fog, and the whole world was quiet. My mind reached out, hungry and alert, into that hush with the sense that great and beautiful things lay behind it.

But the days rushed quickly down into the furor and heat of a busy season. Soon, I was no longer strolling to work but running, usually late, having slept too long after another late night. The days were crammed with people and information. I organized and cleaned, set posters round the city, answered emails, and ran between the church and the various college rooms where all the theological talks were held. In between I read voraciously: apologetics and doctrinal handbooks and scholarly essays. Restless and in need, I hunted down information about God as if I were a detective making a profile of an elusive suspect, learning his patterns and way of moving in the world.

I began to be weary in body, but I had no patience for my own exhaustion. I began to eat haphazardly, to snatch sleep, to walk unseeing past the sinuous river in the early morning. I was no longer beckoned by the mystery of the willows trailing their long-fingered hands in the water; in fact, my weariness began to make me feel that the world in its summer beauty was remote from me. What bearing did trees and rivers and winding paths have on my search to understand pain? What did the summer world have to tell me about sovereignty? I began to become unmoored from my body, and from the world in which that body dwelt. I began to be unaware of God as anything but a collection of ideas, a Being whose love would finally be real to me if I could only collect the right ones.

One day, a famed theologian arrived, the special guest of the summer, and I felt sure that, finally, I would find my answers.

I arrived that morning so weary my skin felt tight and my eyes crusty. I'd had no time that busy week to wash my clothes, so I was rumpled and exhausted, worn out by fighting the obsessions creeping back into my consciousness after too many sleepless nights. I also felt ugly; my weight always went up under stress, and I brought a body with me to that talk that felt unfriendly to me and unlovely to everyone else. I could feel my mind fraying as I sat down in that seminar, but I was so hopeful. I sat in the wood-paneled room, heavy with summer heat, and hoped that this was the place where my hunger would finally be sated.

But the professor began with hell, and before long, I thought perhaps I was in it.

We sped through as many historical interpretations as we could in a morning. Hell as conscious torment for eternity. Hell as annihilation (by rejecting God we ultimately reject existence). Choice after death. Universal salvation. He worked ruthlessly through each version, beginning with those that seemed "kinder" or "soft," but each of these he deemed inadequate, even annihilation itself, because they did not satisfy God's justice. A literal, eternal hell, where God willed people to burn in torment for eternity, was this theologian's grounding doctrine for much of what he presented in the coming days, and what he presented was a system in which an unanswered question was an indignity not to be suffered by a believer.

There was so much information during those sessions, and at first, I tried to be enthusiastic, listing all the bulleted answers in my notes. But I was surprised to find myself increasingly uneasy with the question-and-answer nature of his theology. There seemed to be a direct answer to every difficult question. Sin and evil, suffering and death—these unwieldy realities fit without flaw into his system, one in which God was the only person with any agency. In all my searching, I'd found nothing as comprehensive, as self-assured, as adamant as the answers I was given in those talks. I'd yearned for mathematical answers, and here they were.

To my surprise, they struck at my heart like wounds. They did nothing to bind what was broken in me. They struck a thousand more questions into being, and I felt the little bit of God I'd clung to torn from my hands even as the man on the platform spoke. For the more certain his answers, the more aware I became of my own uncertainty. With a mind as faulty as mine, I never felt sure that I chose or knew God fully on any given day as much as I held on for dear life. And the more I understood the unraveling of mental illness within me, its reach into every corner of my identity and belief, the more I recognized that other griefs like abuse or violence might make faith an almost impossible thing to grasp. What about abandoned children whose only knowledge of authority is of loss? What about those with even worse mental disorders than mine, who cannot tell reality from illusion? How does a system of comprehensive answers include them?

But there wasn't a single question the famed theologian would allow to remain unanswered, for to him, knowledge was all. We could only operate on what we could observe and deduct. Where there was ambiguity, he assumed not love (for this is a divine and measureless thing), but justice (a thing far more easily outlined). God was nailed down neat and hard into the crisscrossed boards of his intricate system. I should have rejoiced since this had been my mode of search. I should have sat back, sated and at peace. But I walked out of the seminar that afternoon with an angry and broken heart and did not return. I spent most of that night sitting on my bed, trying to decide which was better: to believe in the God presented by a theology of comprehensive answers, or to leave off belief in God altogether.

I was so full of knowledge, there was no more room for love.

———

"Beauty, ah beauty,"[2] exclaims a character named Lotty in the charming novel *The Enchanted April*. A lonely, hidden soul with a critical husband and a life of quiet despondence, she plucked up her courage to rent a castle in Italy for a month, a daring, quixotic act that shocked her husband and friends. The first morning she stood on her balcony, with all the gathered glory of Tuscany in springtime at her feet, and "she stared. Such beauty; and she there to see it. Such beauty; and she alive to feel it. Her face was bathed in light."[3]

The depth of that first encounter with loveliness works a deep change in Lotty, for beauty works upon her as a ripening and healing of identity. The anxious uncertainty that marked her personality in London falls away, and she becomes serene, generous, capable of compassion even toward the husband she left behind (so generous that she invites him to join her). Throughout the story of her livening, she is emphatically clear that beauty is the power at work in her heart. In its expansive grace, beauty teaches her that love and joy are fundamental to existence, and this revives her verve and her strong will to love.

I've always thought there was an almost theological aspect to *The Enchanted April*, a gentle, enjoyable book but one whose emphasis on the regenerative power of beauty is rather poignant when you consider it was written in 1922, just a few years after an ugly war that devastated a generation. It's a story in stark contrast to much of the popular novels and poetry of that age, whether the fever-bright novels of hedonism and existential angst in Hemingway or Fitzgerald, or the clear-eyed despair of the Great War poets. *The Enchanted April* reminds me a little of *The Lord of the Rings* because both are stories, however different, that contend for beauty as an eternal reality beyond the touch of darkness, capable of renewing and healing the devastated who look upon it. Their authors, both writing in the postwar world, understood that beauty could communicate the fundamental idea of life as still rich with meaning, the future still shaped by hope, to a people brutalized by trench warfare and Spanish influenza and the death of a whole generation.

"Beauty," wrote Hans Urs von Balthasar, a theologian working in the same era, "is the word that shall be our first."[4] Balthasar titled his theology *Seeing the Form*, for in the face of modern violence and existential angst he believed that our knowledge about God must begin with beholding his glory. Beauty teaches us not just that God exists but that he is lovely and good. Beauty tells us that we were created for joy and summoned to healing. From the glory of the Trinity, whose life is an endless communion of peace and love, we were formed, and to that ultimate glory we are being redeemed.

But the word of beauty as foundational to what we believe is a daring one, as Balthasar says: "the last thing which the thinking intellect dares to approach."[5] In a world shaped by the Enlightenment ideas that reason is the only force by which we can actually know anything and power the only force by which we may influence the world, beauty is dismissed as peripheral to faith. Creation and emotion, music and story, the touch of beloveds, the homes we live in, the food we eat—these are reduced to the trivial, the ordinary stuff that has little to do with the substance of belief in a bleak world. But oh, this is our heart-shattering loss, for where else do we suffer and hope, where else do we believe except amidst our ordinary in the bodies God gave us, in the tangible world he made? Balthasar, bless him, was fierce when he said,

> We no longer dare to believe in beauty and we make of it a mere appearance in order the more easily to dispose of it. Our situation today shows that beauty demands for itself at least as much courage and decision as do truth and goodness, and . . . we can be sure that whoever sneers at her name . . . can no longer pray and soon will no longer be able to love.[6]

For beauty is at the heart of our faith. The Christian gospel is not of an abstract salvation known by doctrine alone, but the coming of divine beauty itself into our "injured flesh" (as Chris Rice puts it in his music), the realm of time and space where the bent world groans for healing. Jesus showed us the full glory of God's eternal and unchanging loveliness in what Balthasar calls the "strange and terrible beauty" of the cross, where the true generosity of love was seen in its glory. Where that beauty came, the world was restored, and we glimpse what this means in a tangible way in reading the story of Christ; for where Jesus came, disease was healed, storms rebuked, children touched, sin forgiven, meals served, hunger sated, and death turned backward.

Material matters because it reflects the originating glory of its Creator and housed the flesh of God himself in the incarnation.

When Jesus became human, he made the stuff of earth sacred again. Our physicality isn't discarded with salvation but redeemed. We may look afresh on the cosmos "not simply as 'nature' but 'creation,' an endless sea of glory, radiant with the beauty of God in every part."[7]

Alexander Schmemann, another twentieth-century theologian working against the postwar loss of belief, said that we further the sense of God's seeming absence in the modern world when we deny the fundamental goodness of earthy creation. At the root of sin, he says, is the fact that humanity "ceased to be hungry for [God] and for Him alone."[8] In a world where even the tangible feast of the cosmos has been drained of meaning, we are "hungry and thirsty for sacramental life,"[9] for a world where stars sing and the heavens speak and we are invited to eat—yes, chew and swallow—the very Bread of Life.

O taste and see that the LORD is good.

This, according to Balthasar and Schmemann and a host of other faithful souls, is a literal command.

And in England, up in my tower room, I was finally about to heed it.

It was Amir's feast that saved my faith.

Amir was my housemate—a rather flamboyant Iranian professor of something or other who commuted to London and told exotic stories of the places he had lived. We often shared the kitchen in the evening. While I made budget omelettes, he sautéed salmon or braised chicken. He was cordial and kind, if a bit fussy about his food, and when he told me that he was leaving and wanted me to come to his farewell feast the next afternoon, I agreed. But I had just come from the seminar on (from) hell and couldn't guarantee what state I'd be in by the morrow. *Depressed* is what I was when the afternoon came and I sat, alone, mired in my endless questions, failed by all the answers.

I went down the narrow, dark stairs and into the garden, intending to stay only a minute.

But Beauty found me. God strode across the lawn and gripped me with Amir's hands and drew me into what felt at first like a dream but was actually the first real thing I'd tasted in weeks. I obeyed Amir's invitation. I ate those strawberries and that brie. I drank that wine. For almost the first time that summer, I talked with my neighbors. I shared internship woes with Andrea, a German student. I laughed with an Italian exchange student about cultural entanglements. And I finally worked up the courage to talk to Ged, our housemother, a former nun who'd left a strict, secluded convent to run the house for the summer. I questioned her about a life of contemplation and prayer, and in her gentle, reticent way, she told me her tale. "But I needed to be with people again," she said.

Night grew up as we lingered, a warm, hushed darkness that slowed our breath and rested our bodies. Bugs chirruped. Stars blinked. We chatted to the clink of plates refilled and glasses brimming again. When sleepiness finally came, I climbed slowly to bed.

The minute I opened the door, my doubt and my angst, my anger and my struggle sprang, catlike, from the shadows. I clearly remember the way I tensed. But the darkness passed me by, sliding away down the hall and into the shadows. I sat down on the edge of the bed, alert to a presence that shimmered and sang around me. The silver light of the moon fell full on my face, and out of the blue, my soul was sated and full of love. Peace grew like moonlight within me, a gentle, gracious warmth filling the whole of my being, and I knew the goodness of God, not as an idea but as a savor on the tongue, a touch of wind on my face, the hand of my friend pulling me out of a life in which I had exhausted my body and starved my senses and into the full loveliness of the sacramental world.

God, I finally realized, is not a thought I must think or a proposition I must know. God is the Lover and Maker, the Friend and Creator, and he makes himself known in the tastable, touchable wonder of his world. We know his healing in the fellowship of his people. His joy is what sings in the wind and spices the best wine and glimmers in the gold of sunset. In the savor of feasts, the cadence of seasons, in apples crunched and friends touched, God is known for the eternal beauty that he is.

But it's not just beautiful things that God gives us to satisfy our hunger.

He actually gives himself, and that gift is the grace in which each moment of tangible beauty is rooted. For it is only through the great feast of Christ himself, who offered his body as bread, that life "in all its totality was returned to man, given again as a sacrament and communion."[10]

———

One afternoon, a few weeks after Amir's feast, I got back early to my lodgings.

The late heat of the day had thickened in the halls of the old house, expanded into a heavy silence. No one else was home. I closed the front door and felt heat and hush soak into my skin like water. The heat made a silence in which the whole house waited. I left my bag by the door and began an impulsive wander through the ground floor of the massive house. The parlors, libraries, and dining rooms of an earlier era had declined into shabby, faded rooms now lined with cheap chairs and periodically stuffed with students from various summer schools. They were empty now; the light through their curtains barely reached the gloom of the inner house. I kept on, on, past the last cave-like rooms and down, down into thick, shadowed halls. No light came now, or sound; it seemed dark as evening when I reached a great door at the end of the last hall. It was wooden, as if it opened into the windy outdoors, an incongruous substance beneath my curious fingers. I pushed.

A single flicker of light caught my eye at the far end of the high, shadowed room: not a fixed point, but a glimmer and flow of crimsoned light. I walked toward it, my footsteps a gentle thud on a wooden floor, my eyes taking in an almost forest-like light filtered through tall, deeply curtained windows. The air was not high and empty as in the previous rooms, but thick and warm. I reached the light, a single candle in a red glass cup on a table covered in a clean white cloth, and realized I was standing at the altar of the house chapel.

A great crucifix hung above it. The arms of Christ outstretched drew my sight, wide enough, they seemed to me, to fall on my shoulders. I felt an instinctive desire that startled me. The questions of my summer stirred to life in the presence of this symbol of the faith that had seemed, at one time, such a threat to me. The presence of Christ upon that cross was so gentle, so quiet, he seemed almost a stranger. I was not sure I really knew this caught, suffering man, that twisted, grieved figure with the pierced hands, the red light flickering over his face.

"He's so quiet, isn't he?"

I literally jumped.

"Sorry," said a sunny voice behind me. "I didn't think you saw me when you walked down, so I thought I should make myself known. Have you been in the chapel before?"

I turned to find Emma, one of the house wardens. She'd been introduced to me as a nun but what I, in my lack of technical religious language, termed a "plainclothes nun" as she looked no different from most of the students I sat with at breakfast in the mornings and further, read Harry Potter (something I confusedly didn't suppose nuns would do). She was short, with bluntly bobbed hair and monotone clothing and quiet, pale blue eyes. She rose and came to stand beside me now, barely up to my shoulder, but a presence that seemed almost to hum with friendly calm.

"It's new to you, isn't it—the crucifix, and the whole Catholic setup?"

I nodded.

"I know, it's all a bit strange," she said, standing beside me and looking up at the cross. "I tried to leave several times myself, you know."

I wasn't sure what to say to this, especially considering she was a nun.

"But it's this table that always pulls me back. I need the Eucharist. Every day. I feel as if I'll starve without it."

I looked at Emma's face in that moment, watched her watching Christ. She had sated, quiet eyes, the kind that Edna St. Vincent Millay had when she "looked on hills and woods with quiet eyes"[11] after a crushing weight of beauty had confronted her vision. I followed her gaze back to the altar where Christ waited with opened hands and given body. I saw the plates set and ready for the bread and wine, and I suddenly understood, in that luminous moment, that in Amir's feast, I had glimpsed the one true feast of the world: the feast of divine and given life by whose generosity the world is made into a wedding feast. I had only nibbled on that feast so far, only tasted the hors d'oeuvres in the garden that evening; but the great, returning sense of God's goodness reached out to me in what he made and drew me further up and further in to the true feast God sets before me.

For the bread given to sate the ravenous hunger we bear is God's own self. We do eat him. We do drink him. We breathe and belong, wholly in and to him by the eucharistic feast he sets before us. In the table of the Eucharist, the Last Supper set by the love of Christ, we partake of something that allows us to experience and remember our true union with our Creator. Only in that feast will our hunger be satisfied, yet that is the feast in which the whole world is made sacred again, offered to us once more as communion with our Maker. Beauty too may again become our bread. I do not always understand the ways of God's love in this world, but I've tasted the weight of it on the tongue and the sweetness of it in my heart, a goodness like nothing else I've ever known, a loveliness that roots each moment of *knowing* I find in the larger life and generosity of God.

In coming to God's table, both finding and yearning for the transformative bread and wine of God's feast, I found that my need for mathematical answers to all my hardest questions fell away in the face of the beauty so lavishly set before me. A solid answer is no bad thing, but an answer cannot stand in the place of God, nor fill the ravenous need of an aching soul; and if we cannot answer a question without doing violence to God's loveliness or obscuring the extravagance of his beauty, then I wonder whether that question is one we can answer this side of the healing of all things.

In Scripture, we are given the story of God's presence with us, not an outlined explanation of redemption but a tale that opens in a lush garden and ends in a feast the likes of which the world has never known. Wedged between two feasts is the story of both our breaking and our redemption, and the interesting thing about a story is the way it can contain the tension of impossible questions and embodied answers: that God is sovereign and Jesus wept, in protest, at the death of his friend. Or that God causes all things to work together for good yet cannot be tempted by evil and does not require it to accomplish his ends. Or that the God whose power upholds the world would show his strength by taking on our "injured flesh," giving us his own flesh in return, the holy bread by which our hunger is sated and our souls redeemed. Or that the answer to our eternal hunger and need is to "take and eat" and be healed.

As I was.

As I am.

4

We Are Not Alone

Mapping the Night

Here is the world. Beautiful and terrible things will happen.
Don't be afraid.

> Frederick Buechner, *Beyond Words: Daily*
> *Readings in the ABC's of Faith*

The darkness reminded me afresh of God, and when we arrived, it was absolute, like the approaching death that summoned us into its depths. We drove the two hours from the airport south into the still wild hills of rural Texas where my grandmother, they told us, still breathed. I felt shadow seep into bone and skin, felt as much as saw the last lights of town and city die in the yawning black of the rural night.

When I was a little girl, the huge darkness of the country nights got tangled up with my idea of God, and I sat often in the back seat of the car on the long drives home, as I did now, knees curled to chest, face pressed against the cool glass as the darkness outside pressed back, like a countenance bewilderingly large, inscrutable both in breadth and beauty, too vast for comprehension and so both a fascination and a terror.

Oh yes, the long dark reminded me of God. But tonight, it was cold. For death lurked too in the unmapped shadow, incomprehensible and chill, staining the warm night with angled edges that made the night and my own self strange. My face—weary, doubting—loomed back at me in the glass as we pulled in over the rough gravel of my uncle's drive. Silence as large as the dark surrounded me as I stepped out of the car into the tiny oasis of brightness made by the porch light.

And I relived, in that instant, the almost identical moment of my first arrival in the Texas countryside almost twenty years before. I had been nine years old when my parents took us from a nice suburban neighborhood in Tennessee to live with my grandmother in the wilds of Hill Country. My grandmother had stepped out of her house to welcome us, a tiny figure in the spotlight of the porch, dwarfed by the ocean of night around her. Sleepy and awed by the darkness, I had walked toward her, drawn toward the lit house out of the mystifying black, like the night moths that fluttered round the lamp just over her head.

As they fluttered round my uncle's head now. Garrulous, even that night, when we had been drawn back into the past and the countryside and the dark by Nana's impending death, he herded us into the room where she lay, tiny and shriveled in a hospital bed, her eyes closed, her breathing unnaturally rhythmic. We stood around her, chatting, stroking her hand under the glare of borrowed hospital lights. We spoke to her so brightly, wanting love to touch her in the deep place where she slept. But even as I knelt to stroke her arm and touch her face I felt at a vast distance from her, as if she was already being drawn into a silence in which I could no longer reach her.

Not that I ever really had. I sat there for a long time, thinking of all the things I wished she could have heard from me, or that I wished I'd heard her say. She baffled me in childhood. She was an outdoorsy woman, most comfortable when she was sweating at some task in the searing Texas heat. I loved her practicality in helping me to identify the fossils that littered our limestone hills or pick melons from the madly twisted vines in the run-down orchard or identify the worth of old stamps in my budding collection. The joy we both took in our shared tasks made me always expectant of affection or endearment to follow, but it rarely did. In her work she was close to me, but never in her words. I was in my late teens before I began to understand that in young womanhood she had retreated into a space within herself from which affection or self-explanation were almost impossible. She simply, I told myself, couldn't speak.

And she did not speak now. She had last been wakeful that morning, when they'd told her that we—my father (her son), my mother, and we children—were on our way to her. She breathed steadily, even peacefully now as we sat round her, hoping that somewhere in her waning consciousness, she knew that we were there. But silence gathered about her like shadow. She did not wake, and after many hours, we crept away to our guest beds. At 3:00 a.m., my mother shook me alert to tell me that Nana had died.

We crept, one by one, to sit awkward and exhausted on a couch in one corner of the room with Nana, dead, in the far other corner where no lamp was lit. One person began to tell raucous jokes, as if we were not awake at 3:00 a.m., as if Nana's body did not lie in the rumpled disorder of her last minutes, as if we, living, were not in the presence of her, dead.

I laughed hysterically, briefly, at the jokes as my parents attempted strained conversation. Then I averted my eyes and lapsed into silence, the laughter aching in my stomach, my sight drawn toward the shadows in the far corner. The jokes subsided as the minutes of our watch stretched long, the hospital so far away that hours would pass before Nana's body could be collected. I turned my face away from her, from the person who had departed into a silence I could not breach. And my eye caught the long stare of the night out the kitchen window.

In an instant I was nine years old again on our second night in Texas, tucked into my narrow bed under the two thin, ceiling-high windows of my new room. I had been prayed for, kissed, and left to sleep. But I lay rigid with fear. I read once that bedtime prayers are a preparation for death. Parents never tell children this, of course, but the rituals surrounding the release of the conscious into the boundless territory of sleep prepare us for our banishment into the wilderlands of death. I understood this inchoately even in small childhood, and I think it was why I clung to my parents' prayers as if they were incantations. But I knew it consciously, viscerally that night.

For everything in my knowledge of the world had changed. We had left the house and yard and friends I knew. We had left the sounds and shadows I knew at bedtime. We had left behind a world I deeply loved, whose contours bordered and protected my being. Now all was strange and I was strange within it, aware that what I loved could be snatched beyond my grasp. And if home, why not parent, or sibling, or self? The vast darkness out my window, glimpsed upon our arrival the night before, pressed in upon my imagination, huge and foreign, enlarging the strangeness and making of me something so ephemeral I felt surprised to find myself still there at all. I lifted the flimsy shade and looked out.

And oh, I was terrified.

Frederick Buechner writes achingly in *The Sacred Journey* of the moment when his father's death set him "in" time, summoned him into that consciousness of adulthood that is somehow the knowledge that the clock of our lives ticks on toward death. My own such moment came, I think, in the instant I stared out at that night, aware that nothing I knew was safe from change or loss. Somehow, in the small grief of childhood held before the vastness of the night, I encountered my own mortality.

I leapt from bed and ran wildly into the next room. My mother was away, and it was my father who turned in surprise to greet a teary, shaken little girl. We both felt slightly awkward, for such out-of-bed-after-hours events were usually handled by my mom, but he took me on his knee as I choked out something that I'm sure was incoherent. To his profound credit, he recognized that my terror was more than a simple fear of the dark. He rocked me until I was quieter, able to articulate something of the knowledge that had come to me of loss, of change, of all that I loved being irremediably haunted by the presence of a someday death.

Then my father did something that I have never forgotten, something that endures within me, a living image that I can still inhabit, one whose beauty tinges every sorrow I have faced. He took me back to my room, but he did not turn on the light or pull the shade down the timid inch I had lifted it. Rather, he sat on my bed with me and settled in so that we both faced the window. He put his arms firmly around me and, without preamble, snapped the shade fully up, letting it roll dramatically to the top of the window so that the night flooded in, swift as black, sweet water, settling round us as we faced it wide-eyed together.

Held, I faced the darkness afresh as my father began to whisper, even sing I think, of the Love at back of that vast and star-spattered night. He swayed gently, he held me firmly, and his heart beat strong at my back as we faced the long night together. He mapped the night by the story he told of the Love that is the light of the world, come down into the darkness to hold each person alive so that none was lost or forgotten. His words were like a fire lit in my inmost being so that I became distinct from the shadows and safe once more. He bordered the darkness with presence so that it became a wild and lovely country to explore instead of a void into which I would disappear.

I tasted, in that instant, what I think was eternal life, and is no more and no less than love not only defying but radiantly remaking death.

Death. I snapped back to the present, where my just-dead grandmother lay in the far corner of the room, lay where I had been afraid to go, afraid as I had been when a child, fearing that the borderless dark of death might lay hold of me too. But with the memory of my father's arms burning afresh in the core of my being, I rose. I glanced at my dad, older, greyer now, asleep on the couch after hours of watching but present with me, and I crept to where Nana lay. I picked up her hand and held it as my father had once held mine. In the quiet, I held her wrinkled hand, recalling every memory of her that I could, holding her in the whole of her essence as best I could. I was with her, as my father had been with me, and together we looked into the long dark of death.

As we did, I remembered the years following that night with my father when the country dark became my own. I dared more and more often to walk in it alone, sneaking off from the lit yard where my siblings played to stand for a minute, maybe two, in the first lapping waves of the blackness brimming the countryside around our house. I remembered the way that my eyes would slowly adjust until I could see afresh in the night-time, until it filled my sight and was near and sweet so that I began to see the starlight speckling its skin.

Just so, as I sat with Nana, assenting to the silence both of her life and death, no longer fighting her quiet or demanding that she speak, her silence became familiar. And in it, I understood that her wordless departure was like her inarticulate life. She spoke by her presence, perhaps only in that way, but she gave it prodigally to a young granddaughter who also loved the golden fire of the summer days and the ribbed treasures of the old earth. She was simply present, and that was her language and her last word, for she had remained, willfully breathing until we arrived.

Darkness and silence: how swiftly the terror is drained from them by the remaking presence of love. I looked out the window where a just-born dawn was crying the world awake in a thin line of light. I remembered something I had forgotten in my adulthood: that by the time we moved to the city in my teens, I felt myself native in the long, adventurous dark, and I'd walk alone at night with the world expanding immeasurably at my feet. Something untamedly good and unexplored stretched out before me so that I rued the need to return to the known and prosaic, the tiny circled porch light of the ordinary world where my mother called me into bed.

> Even the darkness is not dark to You,
> And the night is as bright as the day. (Ps. 139:12 NASB)

I looked at Nana and wondered . . . *What if the radiance of love transfigures and translates even death so that it is no longer the darkness in which we are lost but the passage we travel on our way to being found?*

But I'm modern in my limited experience of death.

I met it in Nana, of course, and the distant, impenetrable news of the passing of two grandfathers (whom I was too little to know), another grandmother (so ill for so long that her death in my teens came as a strange grace), and an uncle I barely knew. Nana's death began to teach me something of loss, but her death remained separate from my own being: something that saddened but did not touch me in my essence. Susette's death struck more deeply, an early and awful death that stole something immeasurably precious. Yet her death was couched in the maturity of her faith, one that framed and transformed my sense of loss.

The death that has shaken me the most arrived without preamble to knock my consciousness into a new dimension. There were no goodbyes, no final words in this death that made such a difference to me. Only the abrupt plunge into silence and, with it, darkness. Like that of the Texas night, except that now it was the dark of my own womb, a black, echoing oval on the ultrasound screen with my baby—that clear, startling outline of a tiny human—sunk to the bottom like a precious stone in a small, fathomless ocean.

"There's no heartbeat," the nurse said quickly as my husband's and my eyes fixed hungrily, quickly on the image, desperate to catch our joy by the heel before we climbed too high and fell even harder. The tears came instantly, my heart and body reacting even before my mind grasped her meaning. But when my reason caught up, it was bewildered. The strangeness of seeing the shape of a baby within me while knowing its life to be absent left me feeling that my own body contained a vast darkness in which my child had been lost, a darkness in me that was a channel into the greater blackness of death as it stalked the back doors of all the living.

That strangeness remained even after the physical pain had passed. What hurt me most and tinged my sadness was the panicked sense that my baby had been taken into a darkness where I could not reach, protect, or shelter him. It was the fulfilment of every dread of my OCD. Of course I grieved the loss of him, known, cried for the passing away of his story and embodied self, of my story as his mother, and the story of what we had already begun to be as his parents. But worst was that sense of him simply disappearing, of death as, again, an unfathomable night in which what we love is unmade, unnamed, and lost.

The old terror of my childhood returned, my long mental illness returned, and for a while, I hated to be alone. Especially at night. I sat in bed, wakeful with the awful insight of the small hours, and saw that we humans stand brave and oblivious in the tiny circles of our faith. We live in the courageous light of our given and accepted love, but the ocean of that fathomless dark laps at the edges of our being, always waiting to flood our hopeful little islands. We are frail. "I say headache," my husband teased me in the first months of our marriage, "and you hear death." But it's true. And in the loss of our little baby, in his total disappearance from any realm of touch or sight, I saw too easily the possible, perhaps inevitable loss of everything else I loved. We are so frail.

Holy Week arrived just weeks after the miscarriage, and since we live across the street from our church, I could not escape the intensity of worship demanded by the season. I felt dismissive and strangely flippant, as if that great tragedy had nothing to do with my loss. I was learning the strange way that grief suspends things you once could count on—emotion, faith, prayer—as if a massive jolt had tossed your life into the air and the whole of you waits to see what parts of yourself will crash, and what will fall to the ground still whole.

I wasn't angry, merely indifferent in that strange suspension. What mattered the abnegations of the flesh when the flesh that mattered had been taken? How could I face the death of God himself when I was still mourning my baby? In sheer obedience I went to church throughout that week, knowing that as a professed Christian I should be able to see beyond the death of Christ (and my baby) to his rising, that I should be able to say with Martha, standing there at the tomb of her brother, "Yes Lord, I believe in the resurrection." But the darkness is very long. And it comes very close.

As it did in the church on Maundy Thursday. I almost regretted my attendance at that service, with the ritual stripping of the altars at the end to symbolize the way Christ's passion laid him bare. Though I knelt with the others in the small cove of candlelight in the side chapel, I clearly heard the ruthless work of the servers as they stripped the church of altar cross and cloths and candles, leaving it bare and echoingly empty. I tasted the long, lonely darkness of the nave as I left, saw the strange, veiled faces of the statues. And next day I saw the gaping space of the empty altar when I reluctantly arrived again, obedient, for the Good Friday service.

I struggle with that service every year as it is, and I struggled far more this time. The liturgy still felt new to me, for I grew up in churches where Good Friday was barely marked, where everyone galloped toward Easter morning and its crashing joy because that, we were told, was our true reality. Living as we do in a world in which people still die, I always felt this was a rather blinkered approach to the season (not to mention faith). But the wide-eyed wrestle with the visceral reality of death confronting me now in the more sacramental worship of my current church continued to rattle me deeply.

Especially the Good Friday veneration of the cross. Every year I wondered if I was toeing idolatry by joining the line to bow before the almost-life-sized crucifix that is processed through the church after a reading of the Passion, or even, as many, to kiss its feet. There was a part of me that craved the sheer physicality of the act, that wanted simply, childlike, to touch Jesus. And another that found the whole thing ridiculous, perhaps idolatrous, the desire to grasp something that cannot be held. And yet, I always found myself in line, curious, starving for a nearer sense of Christ.

But as I stood in the Good Friday service after the baby's loss I wanted to mock that sense. I wanted to turn from the dying Christ, not embrace him. Death had made God distant to me. I felt that the baby and I were both lost in some kind of darkness beyond the touch of love or comfort. My prayers echoed blankly in my sorrowing mind. Death seemed to make my spirit a grey space in which no voice rang with hope. Grief veiled Christ from me so that he truly seemed like all the statues in my church, shadowed and remote. And when they brought the crucifix forward during the Good Friday service, Christ shrouded and invisible, I felt that I could not follow.

But I had forgotten what came next. For as the procession made its slow way down the aisle, the priests stopped every few feet. And a corner of the veil was dropped. Hand, face, nailed, bony foot. Little by little, Jesus became visible. "Behold the wood of the cross whereon was hung the world's salvation,"[1] the priest chanted again and again as the cross moved into our midst and Jesus became a little clearer. I found my eyes fixed on that figure as it came toward me. "Come let us worship," they sang as the cross moved on to the front of the church and was fixed there in the center of the huge, stripped emptiness that symbolized the totality of death. I stared. There, in the ropy, muscled carving of the old crucifix, the figure of Christ hung fully exposed, embodied, graspable, invading the very core of death's echoing vacuity.

I joined the procession.

My mind ached with the sense of something it yearned to understand even as my feet moved forward, closer, closer to that suffering body now filling the emptied space of the altar. As the line in front of me thinned, I glimpsed more and more of the yellowed skin on the crucifix, the muscled arms, the bowed head, the brutally nailed hands. And then there was no one in front of me and I stood alone, bared by my grief before the stripped Christ. I knelt, obeying heart rather than thought, and before I understood what I intended, I placed my hands on either side of the nailed feet.

And at their touch I abruptly remembered the night with my father when my world was dark with my first knowledge of death. I remembered the feel of his bulk at my back, his muscled arms around me, his hands holding mine so that I was outlined, remade, recalled to form and life by love. I remembered the way that the night became bordered and mapped by his loving presence so that I was no longer afraid.

My hands grew warm on the wood, and there, touching the figure of Christ, I knew that my father's act was only the echo of Christ's ultimate act. The cross was the moment when God himself came to sit with us in the darkness, his flesh-and-bone arms with their pulsing, precious blood wrapped round the whole of humanity so that Love claimed and recalled us from the unraveling of death. The cross is Creator with us, comprehending the darkness by his wounded hands so that it may not comprehend us. Christ on the cross means Love with his arms mapping not only the night but death—making of it a starred path we follow not to destruction but to life. The cross means our father has come to hold us, and no one is lost.

Not even my tiny baby, washed out into the ocean of death.

Holding the scuffed feet of that old crucified figure I knew that my little one had been caught by the scarred hands of Love and was held there living, and that even as I knelt, I was held too. For that brief moment, we sat together, in the circle of Christ's arms, looking out the window of my heart at the vast, dark grief of the last days as it was veined by light and bounded by Love.

And though I was still grieved, I began, just barely, to be unafraid.

The next evening, I stood in the dusty courtyard of our old church, the lithe tangle of spring branches overhead as the Easter Fire was kindled in the twilight. I love the rich scent of that wood fire, the crackled music of the sparks as they dance. I love the friendly mutter and hum of people gathered from all over the parish to watch the kindling. And I love the ritual by which the Easter candle is lit from the roaring fire, its single flame passing to each of our slim candles, so that we may process in the light of that fire into the tomb-dark church, singing aloud as we move, "The light of Christ, thanks be to God."

And the darkness leaps away from us.

In the candle-starred shadows I sat, half listening to the Easter Exultet, half mulling my own eased heart. For it was fear not grief, I knew now, that had held me suspended in my sorrow, unsure that anything was safe. Perhaps it was fear through all the years of my OCD. And it was Love, with arms around my sorrowing heart, sitting with me in the darkness, that now lit a fire within me and drove my fear away. I was not kept from grief and death, or a broken mind, but Love held fast to me in it, mapping the night, denying that sense of annihilation that stalks the edge of every loss. For, "living or dying, we belong to the Lord" (Rom. 14:8 NCV), and every candle in the church burned in affirmation of that fact. Their scattered light would someday be gathered into a great dawn. That's the gospel, I think, though I had never so truly perceived it before.

A tiny commotion in the next row down distracted me, and I looked down to see a mother dive to catch her little girl's candle as it wobbled in the child's small hands. But the child, eyes wide and determined, pushed her mother away, sat a little straighter, and held the candle more firmly. She fixed her big eyes on the light, as if it were a face. She smiled. She swayed back and forth, watching the swish of the flame. She kicked her feet and hummed with pleasure, eyes fixed ever on the fire. She loved the brightness. She saw nothing else.

I lifted my face to the figure of Christ, and as the child that I am, with the child no longer lost, I too fixed my eyes on the fire and adored the brightness. And the words of the Easter Exultet sang round me.

"The night is past, the day of life is here."

5

Love Is at Work
in Our Broken World

Expecting Good

"What is the scent of water?"
"Renewal. The goodness of God coming down like dew."
Elizabeth Goudge, *The Scent of Water*

I saw him first by candlelight.

Across the aisle of a narrow chapel, through the high, arched shadows of the darkened church. I glimpsed him kneeling, face lit from below by the slim candle he held. Psalms were chanted in the shadows around us, echoing off the stone walls, and I watched him singing as I too knelt and lifted my voice. He was tall, with a head of thick, tousled hair, and wore a faded green hoodie that looked incongruous amidst the formal beauty of the Oxford chapel. But the peacefulness of him, the quiet of his hands, the attention he gave to his prayer with a half smile on his face and closed eyes, these were so richly at home in that place of worship that I found it difficult to turn away. He drew my eyes—there was no denying it—yet nudged them back too, his hush somehow beckoning me into the larger silence of the worship.

It was a good first glimpse of the man who would become my husband.

Romantic, you might say, except that there was no locking of gaze, no acknowledgment of instant attraction, and the next time I saw him was in the church kitchen, in so much pain from a football injury that he could barely stand. Thomas grinned at me through a grimace and asked me if I had all the vegetables I needed. Not exactly the stuff of great romantic novels. I had just moved to Oxford and become a regular member of the church where I'd first seen him and its larger community. Once the chapel interns discovered I could cook and liked to do it, I was swiftly co-opted into service as an occasional chef for the big Sunday meals. The fact that Thomas was the intern in charge of ordering the groceries and doing the dishes for whoever was cooking may have heightened my willingness to serve, for I was frankly curious to know more of this tall, green-eyed Dutchman with the kind gaze and self-possessed calm.

Two weeks in, we'd managed several cordial conversations, the shy kind that happen slowly between two willing introverts. He was always courteous. As I peeled potatoes and handed him saucepans to rinse, I found he was a former primary school teacher who loved good children's literature. While boiling rice, I discovered he was an avid reader who loved authors I also held dear, like Lewis and Tolkien and Kreeft. Over the mixing of brownies, I learned he was the oldest of seven children, his father Danish, his mother Dutch, and that he had an astonishing forty-four first cousins. I also discovered that he was beginning what is known as the "discernment" process for priesthood in the Church of England. This meant long interviews about his life and past, essays on his motives and sense of vocation, sessions of spiritual direction and prayer, and a larger process of self-examination meant to identify the real calling of the Holy Spirit. I was keenly interested.

A month into our acquaintance, he came back one evening after a whole day spent in London with the priest directing his discernment. I met him, a little eager and bright-eyed, at the top of a staircase leading to the room where we were both about to join friends for dinner. I asked him about his day. I remember the cast of the bright hall light on his head, the evening shadows gathering in the old cut-glass window next to us, the echoes of the busy street outside as he answered, for his words in that moment startled and halted something that had begun to grow in me.

"My director said I should consider the religious life. You know, become a monk."

He said it with half a laugh, but it wasn't a dismissive laugh.

"I've never minded being single, I'm drawn to quiet and prayer, so, he thinks I should really research it."

I stepped back, stilled. I strove to keep my eyes bright as I nodded, conjured a smile, and managed to make enthusiastic sounds and ask how he planned to research this startling possibility. He told me about a monastery in the north he'd visit, and the extra reading he'd do, then waved at a friend and headed into the room where dinner was on the table and the voices of hungry students were rising in their usual raucous din. I watched him go. Quiet, but with a suppressed mischief

I already recognized, his smile breaking like sunlight for every person he met. His hair still too long but ridiculously elegant. Still wearing that old green hoodie in stubborn, amused Dutch defiance of the general Oxford fussiness around him. Kind. I stood a moment and looked out at the darkling sky and couldn't help a sigh. You don't meet kind, prayerful men with a yen for books and laughter and a sympathy for children very often. But I gave myself a small shake and an inward roll of the eyes as I walked into dinner. Of course I'd managed to fall for a future monk. At least I hadn't fallen far and that was that.

Only later, as I walked back to my dorm room through the Oxford streets all dappled with lamplight and stained-glass windows and cobblestones and shadows, did the dark thought come.

It's just as well. He could never actually love you.

For how could I, with my OCD and insecurity, my faulty body and fragile mind, ever hope to attract a man as whole and strong and good as Thomas? And even if, unbelievably, he did look my way, how could he bring himself to actually choose me once I told him that my life was shaped by mental illness? For my family to love me was one thing; sharers of my blood, obliged to me by birth, they didn't really have a choice. But it was another thing altogether for a stranger to choose me out of all the possible women in the world, all the healthy ones, the girls who'd actually left home and gotten degrees and jobs. The ones who weren't too tall, or too big, with weight that galloped up and down the scales at the least touch of stress. The girls who were strong. The girls who were sane.

No.

Monk or not, the beauty of Thomas would never be for me.

———

I have always been a dreamer, and throughout the dark and lonely years of my twenties I dreamed with a might and spunk that astonished even me. To dream was my small defiance of the darkness, and my dreams were bright and precious things, anguished desires that lay at the core of my soul. A home of my own. A partner to know me wholly and love me without reservation. Friendship that was not strained or broken by the worst life could bring. A shared life, a place to belong. Arms around me, eyes bright in fellowship, a home with endless bookshelves and music in the evenings and a big garden where I was not the visitor but the hostess. The dreams were, in their way, as constant as my illness. The background of my consciousness each day, these passionate desires for love and beauty and belonging fueled my energy and drove my writing and kept me walking forward in the hope of their fulfilment regardless of my illness and its constant diminishment.

But oh, I was deeply diminished, because on an almost subconscious level of being, I believed that mental illness made me defective and, perhaps, unlovable.

I bore that belief within me like breath. I don't think I knew it was there. It was one of those assumptions that came at the outset of my OCD, so subtle and tangled with my sense of disaster that I didn't know to refute it. But every time my heart reached out in hope or love, I knew the sly, unraveling whisper of doubt. Who would want to bind themselves to someone so broken? I thought of love as giving, and I thought my illness meant I didn't have enough to offer; this was a conviction submerged so deeply within me that I never thought to fight it.

OCD was the dark, shameful secret I bore with me into every situation, and it meant there was always a boundary beyond which I could not go in relationship. I made excuses to escape situations that might cause me panic. I brushed off as schedule conflicts my refusal of group activities that overwhelmed me. I told myself that staying home was better, the Wendell Berry thing to do, because I needed something to throw at all the people who kept asking me what I planned to do with my life, something to stave off the devastating shame of my incapacity, my unwanted solitude, my fear that nothing would ever change.

By the time I reached my thirtieth birthday, an almost unbearable tension had grown within me. For even as I clung with one hand to these dreams that made sense and order of my lonely days, I bore that inchoate sense of my faultiness in the other hand, that unspoken conviction that love could not come to me as I was. The impasse of it, the dreaming and the despair and the long, lonely years made a daily tug of war within my heart, one that forced me to deeply question God's power and presence in my life.

What did it mean for God to be at work in my broken world?

I pored over Scripture, trying to trust this beauty-giving God for a future I could imagine but never quite trust. The words of Psalm 37 were my challenge and my torture: "Trust in the LORD . . . do good; . . . and He will give you the desires of your heart" (vv. 3–4 NASB). But would he? After a dozen years in the shadow of my illness, I felt desperate. I wanted God to invade my illness with a breakthrough. I kept looking for him to arrive in some kind of power I hadn't yet seen, to heal me for good. I did not believe myself eligible for love as I was, and the grief of that made me beg God to change me, to make me something other than the fragile self I knew myself to be. *God is powerful*, I thought, *so why doesn't he make me that way too?* But he never arrived in the shattering display of strength that I thought was the only way he could answer my prayer.

106

So I felt betrayed. On the larger scale of salvation, I had regained my faith, but on the intimate scale of my ordinary dreams in their tangle of depression and need, desire and despair, I assumed God was absent because he didn't come in the way I thought he would. I didn't yet have an imagination that was healed enough to picture a power that could cherish and heal me as I was—not discarding what was broken in me, but making of it something precious and new. I lost faith in God's goodness as a personal force in my life, for I was so tired, so very tired of the battle and grief, and I could not see beyond it. I began to think God was remote from me. I no longer expected or begged for his arrival. Such dreams as I bore, those were for an unblemished person I could never be.

For who could love me as I was?

————

Thomas apparently.

The fact still amazes me.

But it was a love unlike any I could have expected or dreamt, one that shattered, with a bright, sweet joy, all my expectations of what it means for God to work in our broken and tangled lives, not after or in spite of our suffering but in the very middle of its tangle and need, to make in the dark muddle of our dysfunction a beauty we could never have dreamed to begin with. Of course, it took Thomas eight more months to tell me about his love. He had all sorts of good reasons for delaying his confession, but I never let him forget that for most of those interminable months, I was convinced he never would.

Yet anguished as they were, those months became the crucible in which the doubts I'd suffered and the anger I'd borne toward God were melted away in the pure light of God's actual

107

goodness as it arrived in my life—more tender and gentle than anything I had yet imagined.

I came to Oxford in my thirtieth year, lonely and honest, afraid that all the things I hoped for were moving beyond my grasp. Coming to England was my scrappy attempt to get my hands round at least one of my dreams. But I was a little startled by my success. That year in Oxford was one of such bright-ness and such shadow that I still wonder how one small heart contained it. I knew, first, an almost shocking joy as I grasped the crazy fact that for the first time in a decade, I seemed to be stronger than OCD, capable of independence. I made it through the usual panic of the first week. The dark nights grew less frequent. The panic attacks were endurable. Two weeks, two months, and I was still there, capable and thriving. I dove into my academic work and a shy exploration of new com-munity. Professors praised my writing. My tiny, fourth-floor dorm room became a castle to me, the sphere of my renewing vim. I stocked it with prints from the artsy bookshop in the city center, filled the shelves with theological tomes and novels, bought flowers each week, and kept a bottle of wine and two thrift-shop crystal glasses ready for the friendships that began to form and the late-night talks they kindled.

But that room was also the cell of a suffering keener and dif-ferent to any I had known, and before my joy had well begun, it was tinged with sorrow.

For I was in love with Thomas.

I didn't mean to be, I didn't even want to be, and the knowl-edge of my love grew slowly as we formed a solid and happy friendship. But it was steady. As I kept the company of this monk-to-be—and oh, we saw a great deal of each other, what with countless big meals to cook and compline services and movie nights and community feasts—I saw something as rare and beautiful as any grace the world had shown me. I watched Thomas as he stood by the chapel door, quick to greet the strangers and waifs who wandered in. I watched him seek out the lonely and unclaimed amidst the raucous evenings of food and music hosted by the church. I watched him merrily wash dishes, tease us all, chase children, light candles in the long shadows before the evening service. I listened to his thoughts on the ancient church fathers and modern holiness and fun while we washed dishes. I watched him pray, fixed and happy. And I watched him quietly leave conversations where gossip or darkness became dominant. He hated what was evil, you could see the glint of that in his eyes, but he loved people with an enthusiasm that enveloped their faultiness and quirks in his compassion.

I had found the one whom my soul loved.

I thought, at first, that my love would only bring me anguish, and for a while, it did. My awful doubt grew powerful within me. There were long weeks when the sight of Thomas was pain to me, because all I could see was the futility of my hope, all I could hear was my own self-doubt.

But love, even the love we bear for another, has a transformative power unguessed by the fallen world, and as my love for Thomas grew, it began to challenge the story I told about myself. For the ache and heartbeat of my affection taught me to question the voices of negation, the story-ending narrative of my unworthiness. Love blossomed within me, a radiant thing for a precious person, and in its light I could no longer accept the diminishment thrust upon me by my illness. I could not unquestioningly accept my brokenness as the final word about me, and I learned, abruptly and with a vulnerability that terrified me, to yearn again for God's present goodness in my life as I was, imperfect and broken yet capable of love, to hope for his power to come in the intimate details of my deepest need.

When I went back to the States for Christmas, I began what would become more than forty days of a daily prayer, one that came to me one jet-lagged morning as I thought of Thomas and felt the grief of the love that was at once both a homecoming and its loss. I sat in the dawn-shadow candlelight of my room, Psalm 37 open before me again, unsure of what to pray and tempted to turn from any prayer at all in my sense of futility. But a prayer came into my mind, a gift, and I offered it back in a whisper.

Show us to each other, Lord. I don't know how to offer Thomas the depth of my love, and I don't know how to explain the secret of my illness. But you know us both, you see the core and heart of us. If we are ever to be together, show us to each other.

First though, God showed me himself: his own kind, benevolent self at work to heal and bless me, and this was vision I needed before I could ever believe or welcome the love of Thomas or anyone else.

At Easter, I spent four strange weeks alone in Oxford. Most people left for the holiday, and the vast old building where I lived was deserted. And oh, it echoed as I walked the halls, aching and alone. My mom came for a visit in that quiet space, and her long knowledge of me, her tenderness, struck open my heart with its long burden. I cried long and hard for this difficult love I bore, and for the acid doubt I hadn't yet confessed. We walked, arm in arm, through the bitter, wintered streets of deserted Oxford, and she drew, word by word, the poison of my deepest fears. I learned to speak the doubt that haunted me, and when I said it aloud—"I think I'm not worth being loved and I don't think God cares"—I knew it for the twisted thing of pain and suffering and evil that it was. I wept, but the tears were my teacher, for I found that to grieve instead of to doubt, to yearn instead of diminishing my desire was to emerge like a butterfly from the cocoon of my illness and fear. Something fragile and lovely fluttered within me, not yet the knowledge of my belovedness so much as the hope that perhaps it was not impossible for me to be loved.

But the first love I had to trust was God's.

"Trust in the Lord . . . ; and he will give you the desires of your heart."

How can you trust someone if you don't believe they love you?

In the vast, grey hours of my Lenten solitude I understood that my doubt had shoved even my Maker away. I thought even he could not love me wholly the way I was, frail and fussy, so weak when it came to willpower, so prone to unfettered emotion. I wanted him to take away the things I thought were unlovable, and I thought he was not present with me in my need if he didn't. But all he wanted to do was hold the whole of myself, need and yearning, broken parts and faulty heart, in the healing circle of his hands.

I sat in the half-light of the huge old window in my room in the days before Easter and found the goodness of God, a quiet warmth there in the shadows that drew me, word by word, prayer by prayer, into an honesty that made me hopeful with the simple trust of a child. I knew the power and goodness of God, not as the violent invasion I'd thought I desired, one to discard the broken side of me, but a vast gentleness that grew up within me, pervading the books I read, speaking to me in the films I watched—a power that came to heal and cherish the

111

whole of me, shattered bits and dreams all together. I spent hours reading, thinking, resting in the pale, wintered light, and I felt God's power with me like sunlight, drawing a seed to reach toward the green and verdant life for which it was made.

I had an icon during that time, propped in the massive, single window against which my narrow bed was set. It was an image of Christ in his torture, a simple, folksy picture of a stripped and grieving Christ wearing the purple cloak and thorny crown of his suffering. The icon was named "the Bridegroom," and as I stared at it I began to recognize the kind of power in which my God comes. It's not one that zaps me away or discards the unstable bits of my soul; instead he died to bind them all up in his love. I curled on my bed, loving that God, thinking of him as I watched the poignant animated film *Song of the Sea*, with its selkie legend woven into a heartbreaking beauty of a tale about why we must learn to grieve lest we forget how to love. I loved that God too as I read Julian of Norwich and came to her luminescent passage describing the love of God for what he has made:

> And in this vision he also showed a little thing, the size of a hazelnut, lying in the palm of my hand . . . and I thought, "what can this be?" And the answer came in a general way, "It is all that is made." I wondered how it could last, for it seemed to me so small that it might have disintegrated suddenly into nothingness. And I was answered in my understanding: It lasts and always will, because God loves it. . . . In this little thing I saw three properties. The first is that God made it; the second is that God loves it; and the third is that God cares for it.[1]

In the tower room, I knew God's cradling of my own littleness and need and understood that his goodness is unfailing to us in our sorrow.

By the time the early summer came with all my papers due and my ticket back to America arranged and nothing settled but the fact that at least I'd continue to study, I had arrived at a new understanding of myself and of my Maker. I no longer believed that my illness placed a limit upon the in-breaking power of goodness in my life. My hope was frail. My confidence shaky. And oh, the sight of Thomas still made me ache. But it also sparked a wry bit of a smile. I teased myself at my own infatuation, and it was a kind of grace, the sign that I had allowed myself the dignity of dreaming that maybe, someday, Thomas could love me as I did him, and maybe God would help us find each other. The voices of profound diminishment, relegating the whole of my identity and future to that of a defective mind, had been exorcised from my inmost world like the demon thoughts they were, struck back by the light of God's power at work in the most hidden corners of my yearning and broken heart.

"The hands of a king are the hands of a healer."[2]

In the beautiful ending to Tolkien's epic tale of Middle Earth, the king, Aragorn, returned after a long exile to claim his throne and rule a broken people. His right to the kingship is clear, and because others had stood before him as rivals, he was expected to enter the city in a parade of strength and victory. But instead of arriving as yet another warrior claiming his right, he snuck into the city by a back door to quietly visit those close to death. Making his way from room to room where the sick and dying lay, he healed his people, cleansing their wounds with an ancient herb, calling them back to life so that Faramir (a young lord who could be his rival) is brought back from the brink of darkness with a "light of knowledge and love kindled in his eyes to say 'what does the King command?'"[3]

Just so does God's goodness come to us amidst the battle and dust of our own suffering, our own long defeat. God always arrives with healing. But like Aragorn, he is humble and meek: a king who comes in through the back door of our hearts not to conquer and raze our imperfections away but to hold and heal us by the intimacy of his touch, his presence here with us in the inmost rooms of our suffering. The power of God is radically gentle, never rough with our need or careless with our yearning. God is fixed upon the restoration of our whole selves and souls, not just the bits that everyone else can see. Yet the very tenderness of his power is something we sometimes treat as his weakness or cruelty because we crave a more visible result.

The healing kind of power is not the sort we've been taught to respect by existence in a fallen world where power just means brute force. We want the swift and the visible: illness zapped away, money in our hands, brilliant doctors, prosperous lives, and conversion stories by the thousands. We crave visibility and approbation and health and big crowds that make us feel important enough to forget the frail selves we used to be. When we pray for God to come in power to save us, we often picture a scenario in which God invades our lives as the ultimate mighty man to banish our frailty and make us something entirely other than we are, capable of the will and force whose lack we so deeply feel.

But God cradles and cherishes our frailty, and that is where the true power of his love is known. I always think it intriguing that in the Gospels Jesus seems far more interested in the faith and hope at work in broken people than merely the healing of their bodies. For I think God knows there is no real healing until our hearts are healed of their fear, our minds cleansed of doubt. Broken bodies, shattered hopes, suffering minds, terrible pasts—they leave us deathly ill with the twisted belief that love can never be great enough to encompass the whole of our story. We feel that we must subtract or conceal part of ourselves if we are ever to win the love of other people or God himself. We are diminished in our own eyes by our suffering, taught to despair of our dreams, to give up our hope that God will come with goodness in his hands.

So God creeps in, gentle, and we know his touch because we are not discarded or dismissed, but healed. He comes to unravel our self-doubt, to untangle the evil we have believed, to call us back from the dark lands of our insecurity. He calls us by name and wakes us from sleep so that we too rise, like Faramir, to ask what this kind and precious King commands, and so often his command is simply to open our hands so that they may be filled with his goodness. For when God arrives as the healer, we learn anew that the anguished hopes we carry are held within God's hand like the hazelnut of Mother Julian's vision. The story he weaves for us, well, it may look radically different from what we thought we desired, but when it arrives—and oh, good is always coming toward us—we will recognize it as the intimate gift of a love whose will for us is always so much greater than our own.

One day I walked up the chapel stairs to find Thomas standing in the exact same spot where he had told me he might become a monk. I was going to walk on by, but he stopped me, looked a bit shy, and asked if I'd go for a walk with him up the meadow. The whirl of the earth seemed to pause a second as I grasped what he was asking. But I looked up, eyes bright and amazed, unhindered by the doubts of those long-ago winter months, and . . . "Yes," I breathed. That was a sunlit day, the light filtering in upon our heads through the cut glass all dappled and golden. When we went for that three-hour walk up the meadow and stopped for a pint at the riverside pub, and he told me how quickly he'd decided the religious life wasn't for him but how his love for me was something he'd treasured and tested throughout the past months, I took a deep breath. And I told him right then and there about my OCD. I looked at him across the table, with those crazily beautiful green eyes of his, and told him I was mentally ill, that the presence of it had shaped the whole of my adult life and would no doubt be part of any future we had together. (Because being the humorously intense, deeply introverted, idealist souls we both were, we were already talking about marriage.)

He reached across the table and took both of my hands in his.

"All right," he said. "Let's pray and keep walking."

I was both startled and grateful at this easy acceptance of my confession. I was a little uneasy lest he get home and think it over and come back to call the whole thing off. I barely slept that night in my exultation and bewilderment. The love I had borne so long with so little hope had ripened to something so sweet I could have wept for gratitude. But there was a niggling voice within me that wondered what would happen when he saw what my illness really meant.

A few weeks later, as we walked the lovely streets of quiet Oxford in the lamplight of a summer evening, the inevitable happened. As we went, I felt the whir and shadow of an OCD episode growing within me. That crazy ratcheting of my pulse, that sense of fear at all the unknown ahead, and with it, that suffusion of hot, prickly shame. I panicked, and all the old doubt clamored for entrance to my mind. I was trying to explain something to him about why I couldn't do something, how I feared his disappointment. I walked beside him feeling my tongue thicken with all I couldn't explain, all the apologies I felt I should offer, while my heart grew heavy with dread over his response and my heart beat so fast I could barely breathe.

He stopped us, and we stood in a quiet neighborhood street, gracious old trees rustling in the wind, kind-eyed houses looking down upon us in our little drama. I watched him watching me, knew that he saw my fear and frustration. Then he did something I never expected. He took my face in his hands, my face that burned red and hot and unlovely with the cortisol rush of my fear. He held it gently and spoke to me.

"Sarah. I love you. You don't have to do anything to earn that from me or be anything different than you are. It's okay. You're loved."

"And he will give you the desires of your heart."

I knew, in that moment, that love was a vast thing far greater and sweeter than I had reckoned in my fear. That God broadens our hearts not just so we will feel loved but so we may trust the love that is offered to us as true. I looked at that man, standing there steadily, unfazed by my need, and understood that his love, rooted in the God whose love held and healed us both, could encompass me as I was, not as I thought I should be. He stood there, the desire of my heart, only he was better than what I desired. His love could bear my frailty and fear. His love could choose me not for the perfect self I wished to be but the healed and fragile and hopeful woman I was becoming. God had answered my prayers with a greater beauty than I had known to desire, and in its granting I was not discarded but renewed. I looked into those green eyes, and in their fire and compassion, their surety and their deep love for little old OCD me, I knew the power and goodness of God.

And the goodness grows.

It's been six years since that evening walk in Oxford, and the other day, Thomas and I went out for a Sunday drive with the two small people who arrived to broaden our hearts and deepen our love. We drove through the downs (what they call hills here in our southern corner of England), listening to Fernando Ortega's album *Storm* as we wound through green hills starred with golden-leaved trees. His song "This Time Next Year" began to play, with those lyrics about a little grandbaby and those who love him showing him "the sun on the autumn fields," and I remembered another time I'd listened to that song.

I listened to the whole of that album countless times on a long road trip years ago. I drove seven thousand miles, mostly by myself, through the fire and light of America's East Coast in autumn with its bright, dappled forests and dark, beautiful hills. I was driving to escape despair, driving to get my hands on hope. But as I wandered, staying with friends, driving long hours through gorgeous landscape, listening to music, that song was precious to me; it fueled my dreams as I sojourned in that hidden season. If I was ever to have a son, I would want to show him the "sun on the autumn fields," hold him close and treasure the river-swift days. Of course, the song made me ache. Marriage seemed an almost impossible dream, as did the gift of a son.

Hearing that song as we drove, years later, I suddenly couldn't speak, my throat was so thick with an awed gratitude. Because there again, the dream came true and the goodness arrived. My husband sat beside me and my son, my wild-haired, laughing son, sat just behind me, staring out the window at the autumn fields, his great blue eyes wide and happy. And the grace of it, the "eucatastrophe" as Tolkien might say of this entirely un-expected joyous turn to my story, was so real and rich I could have wept.

For oh, God works and weaves a beauty we can't imagine. He comes to heal, and it may look different than we imagined, but his goodness is always on its way. Good is always being crafted for us, and we are being led, step by step, into its light.

Incarnational Interlude

> Our Lord Jesus Christ, the Word of God, of his boundless love,
> became what we are that he might make us what he himself is.
>
> Irenaeus, *Against Heresies*

"What difference does the Incarnation make to the way Jesus saves us?"

That was the first essay question I had to answer at Oxford, and I was surprised to find that I didn't exactly know. I knew the story of the cross. I didn't know as well the story of the cradle, of Christ taking on our flesh and living a whole, ordinary life and what that meant to my own little struggle of human existence.

Before then, my understanding of salvation was mostly negative. I didn't realize how profoundly this had shaped my sense of God's work in the midst of my pain. I thought of Jesus's life simply as the necessary condition for his death, and his death was what made the difference to me by settling a cosmic lawsuit on my behalf. Because of this, I often struggled to understand what it meant for God to be saving me in the midst of my mental illness. I understood that I might not go to hell, but what did it mean for God to be at work in the here and now of my broken mind, my difficult body, my many bitter attitudes?

A few weeks of study brought me to an astonishing understanding: a God who dies for love may be a startling theological assertion, but perhaps even more astounding is the concept of a God who wraps himself in the flesh and blood, the sweat and tears of human embodiment and by inhabiting it, reveals the beauty for which it was created. Christ didn't come just to settle some cosmic score with death; he also came to show us, in his own flesh, what humanity was intended to be and what it will again become by his grace.

The incarnation means that the life of the world began all over again in Jesus, and no part of our existence is left out of his redemption. What that means for us, what it meant for me, still struggling with OCD, still single and sick and edgy as I studied in a drafty Oxford library, is that redemption isn't something that will happen someday. To be saved doesn't mean to be evacuated from this body and this world and all the imperfect people within it. It means that all these things will be transformed as the life God intended us to have from the dawn of creation is restored to us in Christ.

To be saved means that, as Sam Gamgee said, "everything sad is coming untrue."[1] It means that salvation invades our lives as they are, here and now, shattered, difficult, tangled, and confused. Salvation is static in that it means that God has settled the ancient score once and for all. But it is also dynamic and active, a force of love invading the everyday and reclaiming the landscape of our bodies, our homes, our relationships, our minds, a power that both transforms and invites us to be part of the work that Love does in the world.

Make no mistake, redemption is local.

Our ordinary is where the kingdom of heaven comes.

Unless we understand this, we will think of salvation as abstract and distant, a thing of end times and someday kingdoms rather than the power of God at work to renew creation in our own troubled times, our own little spaces of home and work and worship. We will think it requires no action or courage from us. But the incarnation means that no aspect of existence is exempt now from God's presence. No corner of our lives can be left outside his mercy. The food we eat, our use of the world, the justice we bring, the art we make, these are the spaces in which the potency of God's grace shows plainly in the lives of those who love him.

Our humblest moments are the spaces in which God's reign returns to earth, and I believe that the beauty we claim and create in response to that in-breaking life can be a radical defiance of evil. We are called to courageous creation, for the making of beauty is our gentle and holy defiance of the forces of disintegration and the powers of darkness.

Every kind word spoken, every meal proffered in love, every prayer said can become a feisty act of redemption that communicates a reality opposite to the destruction of a fallen world. Here, in ordinary time, in the kitchen and slightly messy bedroom with a thousand things to do, we counteract despair with laughter. In place of destruction, we make order. We form spaces and hours in which people can be loved and conversations had, times in which those who take part know their lives to be precious. We take what is broken and heal it, giving ourselves in whatever love we have as the answer to loneliness, sorrow, and isolation. We look at each human on the street as divinely beloved and use word and act to communicate that fact with a power of love much stronger than the death that reigns in the daily headlines.

We "practice resurrection," as Wendell Berry states in his battle cry of a poem.[2] To do this is not to denigrate the utter gravity of a world pocked by violence. It's not that we don't mourn or face facts or live in awareness of suffering. But we meet those hard facts with a grace beyond their limited narrative. We live so that our workaday, creative hope is a defiance of the fear by which evil seeks to paralyze love in the world. We root ourselves in the risen Christ whose life in us and in the world is an advancing, creative goodness that comes in the tiniest corners of creation as we order, imagine, and fill them with a love that is rooted in eternity and cannot be touched by death.

This is the world we are called to create by the Beauty that breaks into our darkness.

Shall we?

PART TWO

the world it calls us to create

6

Refuge

Transformed by Belonging

Rivendell was . . . a perfect house, whether you like food or
sleep, or story-telling or singing, or just sitting and thinking
best, or a pleasant mixture of them all. Merely to be there was
a cure for weariness, fear, and sadness.

J. R. R. Tolkien, *The Fellowship of the Ring*

The sunlight slanted low and thick into my eyes amidst the
purple hills. I took shelter just inside the door of the tiny train
station near the Isle of Skye. It was summer, but the luminescent, northern air of that place was sharp and cool even in
the gathered light, and I eyed the soft wool shawls in the small
shop next to me with envy. To be enveloped in so generous and
durable a warmth seemed, in that moment, the one true thing I
wanted. But I turned my gaze to the parking lot lest I miss my

ride. I shivered convulsively as the light failed, and I felt again the mix of wonder and apprehension at the fact that I was in Scotland, on my own, rambling from this place to the next, about to be picked up by a person I'd never met and whisked to a little inn I only hoped was within walking distance of . . . anything. I eyed the shawls again as the sense of my existential unsettledness struck deep. To be enveloped by anything, by love or belonging or purpose, was the larger hunger of my being, and I stood there cold and very alone.

I'd been in Scotland a month, halfheartedly researching a children's book I planned to write, camping out in the spare rooms of a few generous friends of friends, but mostly trying to outrun the depression I'd been unable to shake the whole summer. I was in my late twenties and kept making my dogged attempts to overcome OCD and move into a more independent adult life. I'd worked as a mentor for a student program deep in the Colorado mountains, and I'd studied for a difficult and glorious semester as an exchange student in Oxford. Though my anxiety at times throughout both experiences made me physically ill, I'd gritted my way through and found a fleeting sense of possibility. But both came to an end, and when I arrived back at my parents' house with no plans laid for the following year, two rejections from universities and one from a publisher, a sense of my profound failure as a person was so strong within me that I simply sat on the front porch most days and cried. I tried to hide it, but I was a thundercloud of a soul.

There'd been a dark moment on the night plane over to Scotland. I woke from the fitful sleep of a cramped body and jet-lagged psyche. The lights were all off, and I was stiff with cold. Everyone else around me slept as I struggled in vain to pull the thin blanket over both arms and feet. I gave up and looked out the window I'd left open while I slept. The utter black of night stared me down, unlit by any star. I was utterly afraid. Suspended there in the black ocean of night, I felt that I was Walt Whitman's spider in his poem "A Noiseless, Patient Spider," "detached, in measureless oceans of space," unmoored from anyone who had ever loved me and with no good or sure thing ahead. I had no defense to offer the dark images of my illness as they crowded my mind, foretelling disaster. And the pall of that moment shadowed the first weeks of my wandering in Scotland. I felt the dark of it again: the dark of failure and lostness as I stood, waiting, on Skye.

But a hobbit-sized dark green hatchback jolted to a sudden stop in front of me, and a slim-faced woman in an old sweater with dark, curling hair rolled down the window. "Are you Sarah?" she said in a gentle, melodic Scots voice, with just a hint of a smile. "Hop in." I did, and she soon had us flying down the narrow highway that wove itself like a thin rope through the heathered moors. For some reason, I'd been under the impression that my arrival was inconvenient. I'd expected a taciturn hostess and perhaps a rather severe room when I got there. Instead I found myself chatting away to a woman only a little older than me who yet treated me as her daughter.

"You'll be on your own feet for exploring?" she asked. "Why don't I take you by the shop to get a bit of dinner? I'd cook for you myself, but I'm out tonight. But you can eat with me tomorrow night. Ooh, perhaps we'll have sticky toffee pudding, it's my specialty."

I nodded, a little dazed, until she suddenly swerved off the road into a pull-off. I looked out and saw the delicate thread of a waterfall glimmering through a meadow starred with purple and yellow flowers.

"Ooh, it's so beautiful," she crooned. "You must take a look if it's your first time on Skye."

So I did. I walked through the damp flowers and listened to the faint song of the waterfall and did not even notice the loneliness falling away from me. We pulled up to her home at dusk. A painter's sunset of purple and rose brushed the sky, and the white cottage shone out, friendly, in the coming dark. She showed me to a small, upstairs room that looked over an inlet from the sea and out to the far, navy hills. An old stone Celtic cross marked the landscape to my right, and laundry flickered on the line in the patch of garden below me, swaying in the evening wind. A thick duvet waited on the bed, and a tray with china cups, a kettle, and two pieces of shortbread. I sat down, so distracted by the small pleasures around me and the friendly bustle of my hostess settling me before she left that I was lulled into the quiet enjoyment of a moment I'd not been able to manage in days.

At breakfast the next morning, after my hostess had served me fresh eggs and toast, she sat down at the table and proposed I catch a ride with her to Portree, the main town on the island. "I can show you about a bit, and maybe we can share a lunch, and you can walk home along the hills. I think you'd love it." And like a child, happy and suddenly relieved of my own cares and decisions, I did just as she said. I tagged along with her to Portree and ambled into little shops crammed with homemade pottery and hand-knit sweaters. When she'd finished her errand, we found a cafe up a winding hill and shared a lunch, a plate filled with local cheeses and crusty bread and salad, and she asked all about my life and my past month of loneliness and exploration.

She dropped me off by a farm where the footpath home began, right next to a sign proclaiming "Careful, kittens crossing."

"The walk'll do you good," she'd said. I tromped that day, almost long and hard enough to outwalk my loneliness. Or maybe it was that in my lostness, I was companioned by a kindness that kept me company even as I marched, solitary, through the deep, swaying grass by tiny streams, through thick meadows with countless tiny flowers. When I got home in the gloaming—and it did feel like coming home with the windows golden and my friend waiting with a wave at the door as she brought in the wind-fresh laundry—I found she'd made a rich, spicy curry, and I ate two bowls before I'd blinked. There was sticky toffee pudding after, a dessert of a rich, dark cake covered in caramel sauce and smothered in cream. I ate two bowls of that too, and we talked, late and long. She was gentle and curious, and met the difficult bits of my story I told her with a soft clucking of tongue that eased and comforted me.

The next morning, I got up early to go for a walk before breakfast. On my way out, I stopped by the kitchen, cash in hand, to pay the bill for my room. She looked at the money and just shook her head, this lovely woman with two teenage children and who knows how many bills.

"No. You've been my guest and friend. I don't want you to pay me."

I didn't know what to say, I still don't, but I choked out my thanks and walked, wondering, outside. After two grey days, the sky was finally clean, and the sapphire height and width of it—the sharp, fresh tang of the air—made you feel something good was about to arrive. I walked, quickened, skin tingling. The sun rose as I went, and the light poured like swift, glimmering water through the wide fields so that every blade of grass and wildflower was coated in pellucid light. A steady wind set everything near me swaying, a little orchard where small apples gemmed the trees, a tall meadow where two horses walked, graceful and giant, and up through a green field that stretched to the blue bay. I turned around and saw the tiny white cottage on the horizon, where fresh eggs and hot tea waited for me. I was listening to music as I walked, a song from the Harry Potter film soundtrack I'd always loved for the way it captured the scene and idea of light shattering darkness. And I stopped, there on the narrow road, and put my hands to my heart.

In that instant, I knew that light had come to my darkness and it came because, for a few days, a woman whose being burned with the light of God made of her place on earth a shelter for the lost and lonely, for the stray and the struggling. The burden I had carried for all those weeks, of feeling estranged from the world, lost and forgotten with nowhere to go, had quietly fallen from me because I had been sheltered. Out of the cold wind of my loneliness and the rough road of my depression, I'd stumbled into the refuge of my friend's gentle hospitality. In her generosity, in her offering not just a warm bed and good food and conversation but also the way she led me to dwell deeply within the beauty of the island, to be quiet and untroubled, I had been sheltered. I stood in the refuge of her life and kindness, her home, and I looked out from it upon new horizons of possibility and hope that I could not have found on my own.

Her home became, for those two days, an outpost of the kingdom of heaven. In her place, amidst her story, I found myself sheltered in the kind of goodness, in the merriment and feasting, in the hospitality I believe the cosmos will finally know in the wedding supper of the Lamb. Within the realm my friend created, in the substance of the good food she cooked, the spaces of laughter and conversation she crafted, in the time she made for long walks and quiet, in the constant and gentle way she met my needs, I tasted and saw the real kingdom of God as it came on earth, invading the darkness, an outpost of God's world-renewing life.

———

What does it mean for God's kingdom to "come . . . on earth as it is in heaven" (Matt. 6:10)?

I believe that the beauty we find in suffering calls us to answer that question in embodied ways. The beauty that breaks into our darkness is not a passive grace that falls away from us once we have been propped up and patted on the back. The beauty is living, a person reaching out to us in hands clothed in the very stuff of our mortality, and it restores us not to passive ease but to active creativity, to the generative love that is at the heart of the Trinity.

For in the glimpses of beauty that come to us in our darkness, we witness not just the kindness of God but the nature of reality, and it is *lovely*. The ground of being is, as David Bentley Hart writes, "intrinsically delightful."[1] In the image of this generous and lovely community we were made; to fellowship with this beauty we are redeemed. God makes us like himself, and as he does, our own lives and stories become an embodiment of his great loveliness so that we become, in our turn, the very places where the grieved and lost taste his great reality. In the crafting of the spaces we inhabit, the stories we form within the circle of time, our lives become the shelter where others may "taste and see" the same beauty that drew us out of our darkness and into the light of hope.

God's people have always been people of place. We were crafted first for Eden, God's own garden filled with the ancient

133

wonders of an unfallen world. This was our first home, a realm where the beauty of God reigned so wholly that to walk amidst it was to know the contours of his own infinite soul. We belonged and were at rest, rooted and safe in a surety we've been craving ever since the fall. We were made for home, and one of the first commands God gave the people newly created in his image was simply to rule and subdue (order) the good earth that was their home. In this ruling (a word that too often has been misunderstood to mean owning) of the world, they were to act exactly as God had acted in creating it for them: ordering, nourishing, and clearing a space where new life and love could flourish. One of the first consequences of sin and suffering in the world was the loss of belonging, the loss of the precious *place* for which humanity was created. It was the loss of home, and to be wanderers in the vast and distorted world was the essence of what it meant to be separated from God.

But God, in his way, is a homemaking God, and his action is always incarnational, always involved with the stuff of people and their places. For to invade a fallen world, he made a covenant first with a person, then a nation, and then rooted that nation in a specific piece of earth with a city meant to image the eternal city of God. There is a marvelous and peculiar emphasis on *place* throughout Scripture, the interwoven nature of home and spiritual life so that the keeping of one's physical place became an intimate part of spiritual identity and vocation. The temple was where the Spirit of God dwelt amidst his people, and when Moses was given commands regarding the vestments of the priests and the outfitting of the temple, he was told to make the garments rich and gorgeous. "For glory and for beauty," God said, because God is beautiful and this was the place where people would look to see what kind of God he was.

This national particularity was transcended, however, when Christ came, the very Word made flesh, calling the whole world to himself. No longer was God's presence and beauty bound to a particular place, enclosed in the inner court of the temple. Rather, the Spirit of God walked abroad in human flesh, and where Jesus went, heaven was. Where Jesus went, the cosmos was reclaimed for love. Where Jesus went, people were fed and bodies were healed and creation made whole. Where Jesus was, the earth seemed to be made a home again, yet Jesus spent a great deal of time convincing the Pharisees that God's Spirit was not enclosed in a certain set of rules or pile of bricks. But this never meant that place was no longer sacred. Rather, Jesus began a new reality, a redemption not just of one portion of the world but of the cosmos in its entirety.

Too often, Christianity has taught an incomplete theology of incarnation and place. We have thought that the coming of Jesus meant that no place was sacred and that the fallen world was a disaster from which we would someday be evacuated. This kind of thinking has allowed a disengagement with material reality, with home and place, with earth and body, that has too often meant that the very people made by Creator God are the ones who least value and nourish his creation and are least at home within his world.

But the coming of Jesus, "God with us," kindled the renewing of the cosmos so that all places are now to be reclaimed, all the world is sacred: "crammed with heaven," as Elizabeth Barrett Browning would say. The great invasion has begun. Where the Spirit of Christ is, active and alive within his people, the world is remade and eternity is drawn into time. For the same Spirit that called the world into being dwelt in Christ, and that is the Spirit who comes to dwell within us when we become followers of Jesus. We are empowered to reclaim the fallen circles of existence and draw them back to health and beauty, just as Jesus did when he healed sick bodies and fed hungry stomachs, calmed storms, and turned all our fallenness backward.

We are now the people not only of lost Eden but of the New Jerusalem, the eternal and tangible city, the actual destination to which the whole of our redeemed stories is leading us. Though we are still enmeshed in time, we already stand in the broader light of eternity because we are indwelt by the living Spirit of the Creator. Our own lives and stories become outposts of heaven when the shape and substance of our living enfleshes the beauty of God.

By its very nature, the presence of Christ in our lives assumes a concrete and particular power. Jesus was born in Bethlehem, a real little baby in an actual manger. That humble bed of stone crammed with the musty softness of old hay became one of the first places on earth where the stuff of the fallen world was caught up in the broader life of eternity. As are the ordinary spaces of our own lives: the rooms, tiny or vast, where we sleep and eat and argue and cry, the spaces into which we invite others or raise our children or love our spouses. Here, in the midst of our most profound ordinary, is where heaven invades, where eternity slips into time and the stuff of our normal lives, as we mold and claim it, becomes the very substance of Love.

I have known great homes.

I've known homes whose spaces were a room in God's own house where healing had sway and righteousness reigned. To eat there was to be joyous in feasting. To sleep there was to be safe. For there, as Goldberry told Frodo when he sheltered for the night in her cottage right on the edge of the wild and dangerous wood, "nothing passes window here save moonlight and starlight and wind off the hilltop."[2] The size of the rooms or the fanciness of the fixings didn't determine the power of these places; the soul of the host did, the soul of a person irradiated by Christ, driven to embody their life in the stuff of their ordinary and to offer it to me, one of the many wanderers in the world.

I've known a bit of heaven in a small cottage in Kentucky in a mining town forgotten by the world. I tasted a bit of the Lamb's supper in homemade coconut pie eaten at an old kitchen table set in a bay window that looked out on the dogwoods planted by a young mother long years before. I knew home in the wind-crisp freshness of air-dried sheets, in the creak of old floorboards, and in the fire of a cardinal hidden amidst the yellow flames of forsythia out the window.

I've known it in a cramped flat in Moscow under an iron-grey sky, amidst dirty streets and weary-eyed people. I tasted it, strange but real, in a dish made of bananas and ham and served with verve on old pottery dishes. I knew the fellowship of the ages in the laughter of the children gathered in a room barely big enough for us all to sit in.

I've known it in a great, gracious house in the Rocky Mountains where each person was greeted with a crammed tray full of Austrian pottery and home-baked goods, where tea and prayer opened and closed each visit.

I've known it in a rambling house near the Smoky Mountains, in the stacked treasures of a huge library full of the soul-forming stories offered to any who will come to sit, explore, and read.

I've known it in a long, low cabin in Australia with just a few rooms, where all the children slept in the loft and all of us gathered daily on the narrow back porch to eat vast salads and homemade bread, to speak of aching things and listen to the call of the cockatoos at the far end of the garden.

And I've known it in the home of my childhood, in the birthday breakfasts of cinnamon rolls and tea, in the candlelit evenings, and in the space made for long, wandering walks and deep talks—the rooms formed to shelter the lost and lonely.

But I've also known the fierce battle, the aching work it is to wrest a corner of earth back from brokenness and fill it with light.

For oh, it is always a battle. In a broken world where evil is at work to unravel every good thing begun, where we come to our homemaking with histories of rejection, loneliness, and loss, the work it takes to claim a piece of earth and by our love and effort bind it to heaven is one of the hardest labors of human life. Make no mistake, it will be a fight. For the world Christ came to redeem is the stomping ground of a live, intelligent darkness, and when we plant a flag and claim a piece of it for the reign of Beauty, we've spat in the face of the devil. To be a homemaker is a defiant act because it is work entirely opposed to the forces of evil.

In his quiet and life-shaping novel *Hannah Coulter*, Wendell Berry tells the story of Nathan Coulter, a veteran of WWII, who returns from the horrors of battle determined to create its opposite. Hannah, his wife, recognizes that the home and farm he yearns to create with her is something to defy the disorder and destruction he witnessed on the battlefield. For, Hannah says, "there can be places in this world, and in human hearts, that are opposite to war."[3] The story of the Coulters' life together has been one of the foundational books of my adulthood, one that gave image and articulation to both my hunger for belonging and the larger significance of homemaking in the renewal of the fallen world. Throughout the story, and their long life together, Hannah recognizes increasingly that "it is by the place we've got, and our love for it and our keeping of it, that this world is joined to Heaven."[4] But she is also clear that it is not our love that begins or confirms the homes we make, and I find this deeply comforting.

For I think many of us come to homemaking, if not from the battlefield, then from the different battles of broken family or profound loneliness or displacement. The idea of homemaking is tinted for us by grief, and the shadow of that makes us wonder how we can ever create what we haven't yet had. I've known, in a lesser way than some, the bewilderment of seeking to create a home when you feel homeless, and I've watched that same confusion and fight in my parents throughout my life. My family moved twelve times before I was eighteen. My parents, struggling to find community, yearning for a physical place where we could set down roots, aching for fellowship and family that somehow never materialized, kept hoping to find that one place on earth where we could be at rest. That, however, has never been our gift.

And yet, where my parents dwelt, home was rich and heaven was close. I knew that as a child, even amidst the upheaval of another move, the loss of friends, the foreign air of another house yet unloved and unknown. I was a child with nascent OCD, disturbed by large changes, and yet, my childhood was largely secure. For the moving van would barely have lumbered away, the poor movers still talking about our ridiculous number of books, when my mom would locate the kettle and unwrap

139

the cups for tea. In every home we lived in, there was art on the walls and music in the air; there were family dinners eaten by candlelight, stacks of books in baskets, and our bedrooms made colorful, our beds soft. Even amidst the aching hunger and inner loneliness of her heart, my mother especially set to the work of beauty. Where she lived, the rooms were lovely and the meals delicious and the space claimed for love.

She looked into the void of loneliness and isolation and spoke home into existence.

But the older I have gotten, the more deeply I have understood that she did not act alone. Now as an adult, nomadic myself and married to an Anglican priest whose work probably means a move every few years, I recognize that my mother was dependent upon God's life creating within her the vision she could not sustain alone. The Spirit who brooded over the vast and formless void at the dawn of time is the same one who broods within our hearts, and the words he speaks within us are the ones by which we act with and in him, calling light out of darkness and form out of the shapelessness of our fallen lives. This was the realization I found richly in *Hannah Coulter* when she, as an old woman, tells her grandson Andy what she has come to understand:

> The room of love is the love that holds us all, and it is not ours. It goes back before we were born. It goes all the way back. It is Heaven's. Or it is Heaven, and we are in it only by willingness. By whose love, Andy Catlett, do we love this world and ourselves and one another? Do you think we invented it ourselves? I ask with confidence, for I know you know we didn't.[5]

All that's required of us refugees of the broken cosmos is a willingness to come home. To be made welcome by God and to let our belonging transform not only the inward rooms of our hearts but also the outer rooms of our lives, so that where we are we dwell in heaven, though we yet live in the broken earth— our lives a refuge for the sorrowing in hungry search for love.

———

I bought one of those shawls I saw at the station that first chilly day on Skye. With the money my friend would not take, I got myself one of those generous woolen wraps as the sign and portent of the shelter I had found. By love, I had been made at home in the world again, and the whole of my being stretched in waking, ready to create a refuge in my turn to reflect the beauty of Skye and the woman who made it a home to me. I had little to offer, single and unstable, jobless wanderer that I was. But I set out a picnic of oatcakes and strong cheddar on the train seat and pulled the woolen wrap close round me. In its shelter I began to dream of the home where some other soul might come some evening, lost and aching, perhaps to draw the woolen warmth round their own shoulders, the first sign of their homecoming . . .

7

Cadence and Celebration

Eternity in Time

O Lord, open thou our lips.
And our mouths shall shew forth Thy praise.
from the *Book of Common Prayer*

The sun burned low and crimson above the western hills, a startling orb in the purple dusk as I tromped, troubled and restless, up the wild hillside near our home. I stopped when I saw that sun, awed from distraction by its strangeness. *Finally, something to mark this day as different*, I thought. Different from the endless round of lonely hours at home with my small ones. Different from the past weeks that stretched day to day in unmarked sameness, no friend or event or adventure to alter the sense of time as a vast, unformed space whose echoing vacuity threatened a little more each day to smother my feeble optimism. A red, troubled sun to mark the bitter loneliness of an uncelebrated Holy Week in coronavirus lockdown.

I felt profoundly disoriented in the new world of pandemic-enforced solitude. For us in England, the lockdown orders came swiftly and they felt comprehensive. From one day to the next, church and fellowship, friendship and community, travel and shopping were suspended. We were allowed one walk a day, and I used this to ramble as deep as I dared up the downs. I was only a few months out from the birth of my second baby, my body finally grown strong enough for venturing afresh, and I was restless, desperate for friendship and activity after the deep winter enclosure of recovery in a place where we knew few people, the long nights of new baby care, and a winter season marked by the death of Thomas's mother.

But the lockdown descended upon us the very week when the first round of close friends was meant to join us for a weekend of feasting. My husband, a priest, was catapulted into intensive days of endless work, spending hours staring at his iPad as churches across the world struggled to wrest the internet into some semblance of a shelter for worship (something I'm not convinced can be done well for long). For him, the days were an eye-aching blur of details and screens; for me, hours of intensive interaction with small people as I gave up any expectation of solitude or writing and struggled to contain my anxiety. We were safe and blessed in so many ways, but loneliness grew large around me, as did a sense of the coming months as empty. It felt a little like the first months of my worst OCD—when prayer became almost impossible, when normal life seemed emptied of hope. Everything was canceled, the future suspended, and amidst the days unshaped by any event or friend, I found myself immersed in a deep sense of isolation, wading through a vast, grey space that was time emptied of meaning.

My loneliness was keener that evening, for it marked what should have been a night of celebration: Holy Saturday, when for five past years I'd stood wide-eyed in the dusky shadows of our churchyard to watch the priests kindle a crackling glory of a bonfire from which they lit the great Paschal candle, the symbol of the risen Christ. To watch the Easter Fire burn in the springtime shadows, to light my small candle from it and know that resurrection fire belonged intimately to me and invaded the inward spaces of my own darkness, was visceral joy within me. That great service always ended with champagne and laughter and the Easter feast to come and long days after when our worship and prayer proclaimed a death-defying joy. To live that drama each year had brought deep healing to me.

One of the things I lost in OCD was my sense of time as meaningful and good. I also lost any sense of prayer or worship as a space of God's actual meeting with me amidst the ordinary round of my struggle. When my illness was at its worst, the passing of time was a torturous thing, marked only by the imagery of my worst fears. Time was, too often, a horror—a vacant space my brain wanted to fill with images of disaster or anxiety. I couldn't pray. I dreaded evenings because exhaustion meant I had fewer resources to resist my thoughts. Mornings were grim as I woke weary from torturous dreams. I endured existence, and this meant that my sense of time as a place of creativity and hope was stolen; time became an endless spinning of single-unit minutes, disconnected from any larger good or foundational hope.

While certainly that sense had eased with the passing years and my growing capacity to wrestle well with my illness, I often hungered for some greater scaffolding for the passing of my hours and days and years. I bore a sense deep within myself that there must be a way to hallow time, to make it rich with meaning, but I didn't grasp this fully until I moved to England and began to worship in the older tradition of the Anglican liturgy. For me, it was a revelation: an immersion in worship as something that shaped and redeemed time, and prayer as my tethering to God's story in the world.

My discovery began with a random invitation to attend a compline service my second week in England. I walked, curious, into a darkened chapel where I was given a lit candle. I took my place in the old high-backed pew and watched the shadows flicker and dance over the cross at the altar. A gentle chanting began and I joined in, praying Psalms, singing hymns, chanting the prayers for protection and comfort said before sleep. And I was awed—by the beauty of it, by the way it took the most fearful spaces of approaching night when sleep is a kind of dying, a time I usually dreaded, and made it a place where the peace of Christ came, like warm air through a window.

That single service began a revolution in my devotional life. In the liturgy and hush, the claiming of each part of the day as God's, I recognized a way of worship and embodied devotion that I had hungered to find my whole life. Even with papers to write and deadlines looming, I began to attend as many of the daily services as I could. I'd walk down the road to the chapel, watching my breath in the chill air, and slip into the morning service. The words of morning prayer fell like drops of water onto the cool surface of my sleepy mind, rippling out to wake and gird me for the day. Or I'd slip into evening prayer as the shadows clustered like dark birds under the pews, and we whispered the night prayers for protection, the words a kind of starlight blossoming in the mind. Even when I stayed in my dorm room up a high tower, I began to pray at the set times when others would be praying too. A kind tutor gave me an old *Book of Common Prayer* with a battered maroon cover and tattered seams. He was sorry for its shabbiness, but I liked its age. It meant other hands than mine had loved it before. "Read this," he said. "Study it, use it now and then in your devotions, and you will understand a lot simply by way of worship."

So I did. I kept it on the windowsill next to my bed and began to say the confessions at night, the Psalms and collects early in the morning. I found the words a strengthening frame to my old rhythms of Scripture and personal prayer, and I watched as the liturgies began to influence my thought. I found stray words of them bringing peace and form to the tense moments of my day. I found them most often when I was alone, an echo in the mind that filled the moments that might be lonely with a sense of God's presence shaping and filling my solitude. But perhaps best of all, as I joined more fully with the weekly worship and Sunday services of that beautiful chapel, I began to experience time itself as caught up in the story of God. Days and minutes, hours and years, evenings and mornings: they weren't neutral or vacant, the meaningless stuff of the ticking clock. They were a created space in which God's goodness danced, a realm of his own creation filled by his mighty acts and invading beauty.

In the daily prayers that tethered the open and close of the day to God's love, I was given words by which to proclaim the whole of my life as woven into God's purposes. I did not pray alone now; I prayed the words spoken by countless faithful through the ages. I was given the dance and cadence of the church year, with each Sunday and feast day a space in which I enacted, by both physical and spiritual participation, the drama of Christ's life invading the world, tethering our stories in time to the larger and eternal life of God. The worship I experienced in my church freed me from the enclosure of my lone self in the locked room of my struggle and invited me into the pilgrim procession of God's people whose lives became histories of God's goodness coming to claim and redeem human time and story.

My first Holy Saturday service was, in many ways, the crown and fulfilment of all I was learning. After a week of profound solemnity when each day was a sharing in the sorrow of Jesus's death, I watched the bonfire kindled, I lit my candle from the vast one with the Easter flame, I followed the priests into the tomb-dark church and saw our tiny candles blossom into constellations of light as we sang away fear with the ancient chant "The light of Christ, thanks be to God."

Every year after, I was awed by the beauty and meaning of the act. Every year, I felt the flames reach out to lighten whatever was dark in me. I felt, as I lit my own tiny candle from the larger one and followed the priests into the church, that my own small story was being woven into the real history of Jesus invading the dark world with his love. The solemn, joyous drama of Holy Saturday and its ushering in of the festival of Easter had completed my understanding of time itself as yet another realm where the kingdom could come—our minutes and hours and days woven into the fabric of eternity, our feasting a glimpse of time's completion in the wedding feast of the Lamb.

This was what I mourned as I sat in the red light of a Holy Saturday sunset, bereft of fellowship, liturgy, prayer, and most powerfully, of celebration. I was on my own again, struggling with loneliness and fear, flailing in the great sea of time unraveled by the brokenness of the world, uncertain of any good thing ahead.

I don't think I'm alone in my distress.

Certainly not in my disorientation during lockdown, that sense of isolation and untethered existence that came to us all amidst the suspension of normal life and relationship during the pandemic. But I also think the loss of time's goodness that I knew in OCD is a common one to many in the broken world. Part of what is taken from us by suffering is a sense of our experience as meaningful, of our lives as stories progressing to a good ending. Suffering suspends us in a bleak, grey space of hours unshaped by anything but our distress. Our ears ring with the huge, empty silence of loss and the future looms before us, unfilled by anything but our dread.

We live in an age that further drains and complicates our relationship with time by making our lives a ceaseless round of unbounded activity. In the modern world, we are increasingly less cognizant of the ancient rhythms of day and night, star and season, and less aware of the way those cadences influence our bodies and minds and allow us the boundaries of rest we need for healing. Electricity means we can banish the shadows and extend our days almost indefinitely. Insulated as we are by technologies of all sorts, caught up in the world of our screens, we are no longer as aware of cold and heat, summer and winter as a repeating symphony that reflects the real seasons of our own bodies and souls.

But the internet is the great unraveler of time. We engage it on countless screens, immersed in a virtual reality that knows no limits because it is a realm unbounded by physical or spiritual limits. In grief or boredom, loneliness or fear, we can drown ourselves in the unmitigated flow of its information. But the river takes us nowhere in particular. It is not tethered in a person or shaped by a story. Within it, we may be distracted from our grief but not healed. We can keep our loneliness at bay for a while, but it does nothing to renew the actual spaces of our life as it is, rooted in the earth of a physical body, tethered to the real substance of passing time. This limitless, illusory world does little to draw us out of the closed circles of grief and death and into the widening horizons of real, embodied hope.

I believe such forces increasingly obscure any sense of our humble, ordinary days as the real space Christ invades and claims as his own, the only place where we can "taste and see" the goodness of God. Nihilism, a condition in which we experience existence as meaningless, is a growing reality for many people. There are countless theories and, no doubt, reasons for why belief in God is so difficult in the modern world, but I would argue strongly that one of them is because our experience of time is increasingly removed from the incarnational world where God's love comes to make us whole in a concrete, embodied way.

C. S. Lewis, in his book *The Discarded Image*, described the way that medieval people understood time as intricately related to God and eternity. He also observed the distinctly impoverished modern equivalent of endless time, calling it "perpetuity" or "the attainment of an endless series of moments." He saw eternity as something far different: not an endless string of identical minutes but "the actual and timeless fruition of illimitable life."[1]

We are called, by the in-breaking power of beauty, to the "fruition of illimitable life." We are called to time made rich with life and thick with meaning. This is the call and joy I tasted each year at the Easter vigil when time itself seemed tied again to the ripened life of eternity. And this is the call I have known countless times in my many encounters with God's beauty. When beauty breaks into the circles of our suffering it always includes a redemption of our experience; it sets us again in the river of God's action, in the dynamic movement of the Spirit in which we are drawn out of stagnancy and into the forward gallop of God's good story telling itself in the world.

But what does it mean for us to keep hold of this deep experience in the midst of a broken world? What does it mean for us, in our suffering and loneliness, to join our difficult hours into the "fruition" of God's own life? How can we take the void of grieved days and formless futures and reconnect them to the golden thread of eternity, invading time and weaving all things back to ripened, eternal life?

How can we become a people whose story is shaped by celebration?

I don't mean just throwing a party. Anybody can eat a lot of food and have fun and be entertained. I mean the kind of celebration that is a chosen joy, rooted in a larger and future hope. The kind of celebration that drove the dancing in the streets on VE Day after the Second World War, or the champagne drunk at the end of the Easter service when the darkness has been banished and all of us stand in the light of the resurrection and the world to come. For if there is one thing I have come to understand through the dark days of my suffering, it's that real celebration like that I knew during the Easter vigil is a radical act, an embodiment of wholeness and joy that defies the brokenness around us, an act only possible to a people who are rooted in the wider time of God's story.

In Marilynne Robinson's *Lila*, one of the novels I love most in the world and a story that came to me in the midst of my illness, I found the inner monologue of a woman whose long experience of loneliness and cruelty and loss left her incapable of staying anywhere for long. She was nomadic, unshaped by any sense of the future, unwilling to be caught. Her past was so deeply shadowed by painful memories that it unmoored her sense of time, leaving her incapable or unwilling to live by any hope in the future. In the beginning of the book, she comes to the reader as the product of "an endless series of [destructive] moments."[2] But the tale of *Lila* is of a soul being drawn out of loneliness and into the light of love, into a sense of time, the understanding of her life as a story with the possibility of grace ahead. One of the moments of real redemption in the book comes when Lila stands in the kitchen of the man she has married, whose great love for her is the force reaching out to heal and remake her wounded heart. Before this scene, she has always toyed with the possibility of leaving him. But standing there, hand over her pregnant belly, she begins to imagine the future, to picture a time ahead when her son will be born, and in her heart she speaks to him, thinking,

> If we stay here, soon enough it will be you sitting at the table and me, I don't know, cooking something, and the snow flying, and the old man so glad we're here he'll be off in his study praying about it. And geraniums in the window. Red ones.[3]

The passage describes a reorientation of her whole inner world as she becomes capable of imagining a future with hope and love. The strength of that image renews her sense of time as capable of bringing her good things, of drawing her forward into blessing, which in turn hallows and heals her experience of the present: not as a place she can't wait to leave but as a space in which the beauty of her love can grow and take literal shape in a windowsill full of flowers.

This is, to me, an image of what it means to have our sense of time restored after sorrow.

What we need is the healed capacity to imagine and believe the profound goodness of the future, to stand in the light of a happy ending whose power reaches into our present and draws us forward in hope. For we too have a Husband whose love transforms our story. From the earliest days of Christianity, followers of Jesus have understood that worship is a "resacralization" of time. By entering time, Christ owned and redeemed it, redirecting our disastrous progression to death toward, instead, the dawning horizons of eternity. To be a Christian is to embody this knowledge in the days, hours, and minutes of our lives—the high and holy days of worship and the lowly and precious space of the breakfast table.

I studied the Celtic Christians in the early days of my discovery of sacramental worship and found this powerful description for what time could be to those who formed their lives on the rhythms of worship: "The year was a microcosm of the whole faith: a sequence of sacred periods that recalled the key moments in the mystery of Christ" so that those who worshiped were drawn into Christ's own story, "praising God with the inhabitants of that higher world: the angels and powers, the cherubim and seraphim, the choir of the apostles and prophets."[4]

The Celtic Christian was always in two worlds, the seen and the unseen divine, and in many ways, it was through their worship and the celebrations of the church year that they "journey[ed] along the edge" of time and eternity. These early Celtic believers understood the prayers and celebrations of the church as a "dance" to be joined in time. The Christian's task was to "enter into it and be absorbed within it,"[5] to allow the disciplines of prayer and fasting, worship and feasting to shape their experience and use of earthly time so that it became the place where Christ's kingdom continued to invade the broken world.

What I love about the Celts is the way they understood worship as intimately involved with the ordinary. It wasn't just a thing for high and holy days, it was the cadence by which you woke and worked, slept and ate. This understanding gave rise to a body of ancient prayers spoken by the Celtic peoples and passed down mother to daughter, father to son. In the nineteenth century, a researcher named Alexander Carmichael gathered as many of these blessings as he could, often transposing them for the first time from the mouths of people who'd said them for centuries. Called *The Carmina Gadelica*, the book of blessings is rich in a sense of each day and act as tethered to the story of God. There are resting prayers and morning blessings, prayers for aid against evil and in praise to the "lightener of the stars." Prayers for milking and weeding, for floods and flocks. Prayers by which the human experience of time becomes the space of God's blessing and work.

> O GOD, who broughtst me from the rest of last night
> Unto the joyous light of this day,
> Be Thou bringing me from the new light of this day
> Unto the guiding light of eternity.[6]

In the light of such worship "life on earth takes on a heavenly dimension,"[7] says Hans Boersma, a theologian who speaks of the way our life on earth is now tethered to God's life, and the difference that makes to the whole of our embodied experience. For "participation in heaven changes life on earth,"[8] and while the "not yet" nature of the fallen world is clear, our rhythms of daily worship (prayer instead of the iPhone), our pursuit of quiet, our choice to feast in the face of loneliness and to live in awareness of season and light are rooted in the life of Christ, following his incarnational movement in the world. Time, which became a bleak landscape amidst our suffering, is renewed by Christ into a lush, green land where his goodness grows—the river valley we travel on our way to the holy city whose beauty is for the healing of the whole world, where one day, a wedding feast will mark our homecoming.

But what do you do when you can't attend the feast right now?

What if, whether through the indignities of pandemic lockdowns or the isolation of illness or the impossibility of distance or any other number of anguished reasons, you cannot attend a celebration or join your voice in worship or pray with another? When we are alone at home, when we are lonely and suffering, are we disconnected from meaning—from an experience of time redeemed and rich with God's presence?

The answer Beauty always gives is no, and I remembered that finally on the downs that lonely Holy Saturday night.

I watched the sunset, then I began to walk back down when the air was purpled and dim with the coming night. I was listening to music, and a new composition by my brother, a choral composer, began to play. I stopped at the gentle, aching voices singing the Latin words of *Ubi Caritas*. At first, the beauty of the song deepened my sense of loss, for this was an ancient piece written for a choir and meant to be sung in the fellowship of Holy Week worship. But the actual words, whose translation

I knew from past reading, filtered into my thought, and they acted upon me as the gentle summons of God:

> Where charity and love are, God is there.
> The love of Christ has gathered us into one.
> Let us exult, and let us rejoice in the same.
> Let us fear and let us love the living God.[9]

For one swift moment, time slowed as the words blossomed in my mind and God's presence grew up about me. The music, such a rich weave of bell-bright voices and harmony, stopped me in my restless desire and called me to attention. And in the widened air of that moment, I knew: where love is, even the frail love of my lonely heart, God is. His is the love that makes all of us one, gathering us into the church that is his bride so that though we walk in loneliness, we are never alone. We are made for the fellowship of the church, but when isolation keeps us from that grace, we have fellowship with Christ himself. In his love, we are joined to the kings and queens and kinfolk of heaven (as the Celts might say), to believers around the world lifting up their hearts in yearning and loneliness and prayer. Through his Spirit, burning in our hearts, we are empowered to join our days with the larger life of eternity, by our prayer and devotion to enact and claim the life of God for our individual existence. I walked swiftly through the tall grass and the dark, cool air and wondered how to enflesh and honor that reality.

When I was a few feet from home, I saw the flickering of tiny lights through the window. My husband had lit candles all round our little living room and printed off the liturgy for the Holy Saturday service. I walked into the candle-dappled quiet and knew myself stepping into God's time again, drawn out of my angst and loneliness by the gift of that warm, blessed space made by my husband. Within our home that evening, he and I let our tiny candles reflect the yearned-for flames of the Easter Fire. We spoke the words of joyous celebration, of resurrection and praise, and word by word, they pulled us out of the void space of sadness and into the shaped beauty of celebration.

The next day, we made a feast in defiance of our loneliness. We prayed the magnificent Easter prayers, then pulled out the china and champagne. We baked and basted, set out crystal glasses and crisp white cloths. Because though it was just us with two small children, our home was the only space where celebration could happen that year, the hours within it the only ones we had to receive the joy of Easter. We found that as we shaped our hours to receive him, Christ came. He was already there, just waiting to fill and shape, to brighten and liven the hours we offered into his hands, to fill them with his love and root us again in the larger life of his kingdom.

Madeleine L'Engle, writer and luminous soul, wrote that there are two kinds of time described by the ancient Greek words *chronos* and *kairos*. *Chronos* is simply the clock's march of minutes and hours. But *kairos*, she writes, is "God's time":

> In *kairos* we become what we are called to be as human beings, co-creators with God, touching on the wonder of creation. This calling should not be limited to artists, or saints, but it is a fearful calling.[10]

Beauty calls us to *kairos* amidst our pain. *Kairos* is our gift; when beauty breaks in upon us, when we stand astonished and quiet at the touch of music or light, as I did up on the downs that Holy Saturday night, or in the light of all the Easter Fires that came before it, we stand in *kairos*. But *kairos* is also our choice, a way of offering our hours to God so that they become the cup and cradle for his precious life.

We tried, for the rest of lockdown, to live the grace and gift of *kairos*. We pushed back against the borderless demands of the online world and the shapeless sense of schedule-less days. We began to say morning prayer as a family, with toddlers and teddy bears and babies strung about. We limited our internet and widened our reading. We sat down to dinner each night. We lit candles. We said compline together before bed. We took all the vast, vacant time and shaped it into a place where love blossomed and laughter grew. And each Sunday, we set ourselves a feast, a space of time set aside for prayer and joy, for good food and praise: the center feast of a life marked by Easter celebration.

8

Fellowship

Touching Love

I was wrong, everybody needs someone, to hold on
Take my hand, I've been a lonesome man, took a while
    to understand
There's some things we can't live without,
A man's so prone to doubt,
Faithful are the wounds from friends.

                Josh GarrTels, "Bread and Wine"

"When you're scalded, touch hurts, however kindly meant,"[1] says Lila, the vagabond woman in Marilynne Robinson's novel, when love comes late to her lonely story.

And it does hurt. For such a long time, I couldn't bear to be touched. I sat balled into a corner of the couch so that no one else in my big, noisy family could accidentally sidle up against me. I wrapped my arms tight round myself in social situations.

When people, unknowing, hugged me, or my family clumped round me unaware of my fear, I sat rigid, striving to keep myself separate. Even the squeeze of my mother, a touch I knew as well as my own skin, made me stiffen. The dark nature of my mental illness, the graphic images that came to me so relentlessly, made me afraid that I might contaminate anyone I touched. Deep introvert that I was, I doubt I ever said out loud, "Don't touch me." But I drew back, avoiding affection, unsure any longer of how to give or receive it. Eventually, affection even made me angry. I struggled with God's distance, I ached with my own guilt and confusion. I thought I no longer wanted anyone to touch me, for it implied an innocence I no longer felt or the invitation to a vulnerability I couldn't give.

I thought I wanted to be left severely alone, for my own sake, and the safety of everyone else.

Soon after my diagnosis with OCD, we moved from the high splendor of the Colorado mountains to the close, humid countryside near Nashville, Tennessee. It was a hard move, the loss of the sky and pine-blessed house that had felt like the home we'd finally never leave, a move couched in my many struggles and my parents' intricate difficulties in ministry, not to mention the complicated emotions of three displaced teenagers and their eight-year-old sister. We now lived down a narrow, winding highway deep in the country, in a welcoming but wolf spider–haunted house that backed up to a farmer's field.

There were times when it was a strangely gorgeous place and hope seemed to sit again on the doorstep; in autumn when the leaves burned and the days mellowed and we spent hours down by the lake we could reach by tromping through the fields, when we read together and brewed hot chocolate and glimpsed belonging. But there were long months of ever-deepening loneliness too as the difficulties of the season piled up: financial stress and a back injury, illness and isolation. We found we had moved too far out from the places and people we knew in the city to have any real communion with them, and the isolation began to settle, cold and unshakable, upon us.

In the midst of this, I drew deeply into myself, for my illness had, for then, ended any dreams of university or independence at that time. My body, worn out by the stress and anguish I had hidden for months, began to fail. I gained weight, face flushing weirdly, heart beating wildly, with something no doctor could quite diagnose. I thought myself entirely undesirable on any level, a sense that doubled as my friendships began to unravel. The eyes of my oldest comrades grew cool and careful at my attempt to explain what it meant to wrestle with a broken mind. The movie *A Beautiful Mind*, the story of the brilliant, schizophrenic scientist John Nash, had just been released, and I watched it with my dearest friend, hoping it would help me to explain. "But that's just weird," she said.

My sense of isolation was increased by my growing awareness that my parents could not save me. With deep grief, I recognized that they felt profoundly helpless in the face of my illness, that it was a mighty darkness that came on the heels of other shadows, sometimes too great for them to bear. I came upon my mother one night, grieving by candlelight in the darkness of her bedroom, and knew, abruptly, that she too was liable to breaking, that she was as terrified, in her own way, as I was—her life in as great a turmoil as my own.

And so, for a while I was very alone and began to cultivate my isolation as my shield. I pondered life and the fact that it seemed largely struggle, and I drew myself up into a fortress. I'm sure I was as moody a teenager as they come, yet I also fought against allowing too much emotion out. Having read as much as I could about how to manage my OCD, I began to practice the basic tenets of cognitive behavioral therapy, confronting my dreaded thoughts with firm rejection. On some level, it helped; on another, it required a steeliness in me that only made my fear of vulnerability worse. Because I felt at ease there, I withdrew often to the shadows of my room—a converted garage with a window looking up into a low hill of crab apple trees that made a pink canopy over my bed in spring and a lacework of branches through which I glimpsed the stars in winter. In between avoiding the wolf spiders, I sat on my bed with books or journal, angrily rejecting the images that never ceased to invade my brain, trying to imagine what my future might be, what would happen to all of us, mired there in the country and in our loneliness.

One time though, I woke in the small, black hours of deepest night. The silence was thick as mud; I struggled to breathe, and the dream from which I'd woken, tinged with all the worst images of my OCD, still echoed in my imagination. I was terrified. I was disoriented, incapable of resisting the scenes that began to crash into my mind, unable to think or reason myself out of a sudden sense of profound spiritual isolation. My fierceness fell away. In the face of that darkness, in the larger darkness of my illness and the void future, I felt myself disintegrating, and I was a small child desperate for my mother.

So I called her. I was eighteen and ashamed to do it, but I called her, desperate. I woke her from a deep sleep, and she came to me, sitting beside me on the bed in the shadows. I don't know what I said or what she tried to say, but eventually, she did something that shocked me, something I never could have asked for, something the whole of my being craved but hadn't realized until that moment. She turned back the covers and got into the creaky antique bed beside me. She put her arms around me in the darkness, holding me as she had when I was a small child who could fit in her arms, and she began to whisper to me the kinds of gentle, easing words you speak to a fitful baby.

Hush, precious. It will be all right. I love you.

And warmth spilled through me. Oh, it burned; the ache and grief I had tried so long to suppress and bear alone all rose to the surface of my skin, and my fear burned with it, my panic that I couldn't protect my mother from the evil of my thoughts. But somehow, in the powerful grace of her love, none of it could get a lasting grip upon me. The burning was not a static thing but a rush of light like water that streamed through me, cleansing me; and the pain was not of destruction, but of health creeping back into the shocked, fragile spaces where illness had so long held sway. In her arms, in the tight protection of her affection, I experienced the world in a different way.

I began to hope.

My mother's love laid a strange and beautiful claim upon me, drawing me back from the long, dark plains—not just of my fear that night but also the months of my growing isolation. My hardened and fearful solitude unraveled in that hour. The release was visceral and comprehensive. I looked out upon my life that night from the shelter of her affection and understood abruptly but very fully that there was more to the world than I had been able to know alone. There was more to the story of struggle and the future it laid before me than I could imagine by myself. Alone, I could see only the limitations of my condition. In the interlocked presence of my mother with me, bearing the darkness, I discovered that there were other voices telling the story along with me. There were more forces at work than my own grit or despair. I began in that moment to understand something that has eased and healed my sorrow every time I can remember and accept its grace:

Love turns loneliness backward and remakes the world.

It wasn't that my OCD ceased or my life turned rosy the next morning. The struggle was still real. The difference was that I knew myself held and companioned within it. I'd known that, of course, before, but the visceral experience of love allowed me to know it as a real, living power that could shape my story. I was set once more within the circle of affection—one my mother had to drag me back to again and again, I know, but one in whose grace I could glimpse the larger story of belonging and hope. Her holding of me in the darkness made it possible for me to believe that God too could hold me with the kind of affection that shatters the closed horizons of suffering. Though I did not know it then, her love made God's love imaginable to me.

Fifteen years later, I saw a painting of Christ that helped me to understand the power of what my mother's love brought me in that moment. I was pregnant with my first child, waddling around Florence with my husband on our last holiday before parenthood, when I saw Caravaggio's portrait *The Incredulity of Thomas*, the artist's depiction of the moment that Thomas is granted his childlike desire to touch the risen Lord. The image winked out at me in the long, low gallery, bright as a star behind the dozen tourists through whom I moved to reach it. I stood there, mesmerized by the forms: Jesus, leaning gently toward Thomas, holding back his robe, reaching for Thomas's hand, trying to show him that everything he's asked for has arrived. And Thomas, terrified, his bravado a front for his desire and fear, a fear that now makes him almost unable to grasp the desire of his heart.

Something stirred deeply within me as I looked, for in that portrait I saw myself and the history of my struggle.

I saw myself so clearly in Thomas, who was desperate to touch God but terrified to actually believe that what he desired has come. It was the whole history of my OCD and the darkness it brought, the isolation I sought that was the mask for my terror and need. But the more I looked at the face of Christ, the better I understood the love that had been at work, the beauty breaking into my darkness, working in and through the hands of my mother and the other people who touched and healed me with their affection throughout the dark years of my struggle. Here was a love that put itself in the hands of needy humans, that did not deny but rather granted their whimpered requests for assurance, their fearful need to touch and see. Here was the lover baring his heart in total gift to those frail and faulty disciples, crowding round, hungry, desperate, curious.

And there was the love I had touched in the fierce affection of my mother, a love I came to know through her generous act of communion, her presence with me in the darkness. In that moment, I understood far better than I yet had the nature of the beautiful love at work within my darkness and the fact that we are called out of our darkness to bring that love to others.

> Love one another.
> Love one another as I have loved you.[2]

One of the worst aspects of suffering is the isolation in which it sets us. To be in pain is, in a way, to be cut off from the presence and safety of love. Our loss and our grief, our history of abuse, our sense of abandonment, our secret disorders of body and mind: these separate us from those around us and from our belief in God's fellowship with us. We flail in a sort of shadow world where what we knew and trusted as true or good is removed to an untouchable distance. Into this shadow realm comes the hand of God, but it is so often clothed in the skin of another. In the profound embodiment of our stories here on earth, with the histories of our suffering written in skin and face and psyche, God sends his people to touch and heal each other.

We are called by Love to be lovers, and this is one of the great works by which the beauty of God heals a broken world.

―――――

My daughter, Lilian, is named in part for Lily Potter, Harry's mother in the famed Harry Potter series. Of course there are biblical and spiritual reasons for the name we chose, but I also wanted my girl to have a story to ground and shape her identity. I love Lily Potter because though Harry is the hero, the boy who lives while Lily dies, it is her love in which the whole of his story is rooted. For as Dumbledore tells Harry when he explains why Harry (as a baby) was the only known person to escape a killing curse, when Lily laid down her life to protect her son, her love "left its mark." "To have been loved so deeply . . . ," Dumbledore explains, "will give us some protection forever."[3]

I wanted my own Lilian to have the identity and imaginative camaraderie of a woman who fiercely and faithfully loved, for this is the mighty work I believe God's beauty requires of us who have been healed and made whole by his touch.

Can love really save the world?

It's so easy to dismiss this idea as sentimental, yet this is the core truth of the gospel.

Jon Sobrino, one of the passionate theologians writing in the era of liberation theology, when many in the church yearned to live the fellowship and love of Christ in a radical new way, wrote that Jesus came to restore brotherhood (and sisterhood) to all humanity. We take the idea of "brothers and sisters in Christ" so lightly, yet this is the radical, practical truth of the gospel. In Christ, we are made members one of another and owe each other the care and attention of siblings. Sobrino, along with others in the liberation theology movement, was deeply concerned that this familial love, this "filiation," be concretely expressed in justice and reconciliation to the poor and the people who are our neighbors, not in an abstract sense but in a walk-next-door sense of practical generosity.

What does it mean to love as Christ loves, to love in such a way that we make the tenderness of Jesus tangible to those around us?

I was thinking about this one Christmas on a long flight back to Colorado from England. I was alone and seated next to a woman whose fear of flying became more than she could bear about halfway through our international flight. We hit some turbulence, and as the plane banked and shuddered, she began to wail, hands over her face, trembling uncontrollably. She was seated between me on the aisle and a man by the window, and without much thought, we each grabbed one of her hands and held it tight, talking nonstop to her as we did. She gripped us as if we were the two strings on a parachute holding her a few feet from death, and she stayed that way the rest of the flight.

I was startled by the strangeness of the situation, the barriers of polite distance abolished in the face of need and fear. There I was, as introverted as the day is long, clutching hands with a stranger for hours, patting her back, squeezing her fingers like a child's. But as the minutes, then the hours wore on, the strangeness gave way to a special and startling tenderness. In the moment of her darkness and panic, when she was most alone, we strangers had the chance to meet her in her terror not with rejection but with love. With a strong grip and a steady eye, with hearts willing to hold her up as long as she needed our courage.

My mind wandered somewhere amidst it all back to my questions about love, and I almost laughed out loud at the sheer humor and pathos of my answer. For there in the airplane I saw an image of what I think God asks us to do for each other to make his tender love known in the world. Love my literal neighbor, there in the seat beside me; hold her sweaty hand and pass her another glass of water with my free hand and talk my introverted self blue in the face until we were safely landed. To pour myself out for the comfort of a terrified soul, to answer her needs of body and heart, to grip her hand in the darkness with the same kind of love that guided Thomas's hand to the wounded side of his Savior. Just as I was held in my darkness by my mother, made safe and capable of courage by her presence in my fear.

I am so often like the woman in Dostoevsky's great novel *The Brothers Karamazov* who came to the beloved spiritual elder in the story, begging to be taught how to love. She was passionately in love with the idea of her own profound affection for humanity and her capacity for self-sacrifice but felt offended at the indignity of loving ungrateful or sick or needy people. The monk laughed and soon disillusioned her of any idea of love as idealistic or ethereal.

Love is earthy and often dirty, involved with the quirks and sin of a broken people. I find it so much easier to imagine loving orphans than to realize that kingdom-bringing love is what I ought to bring to the changing of diapers and the rocking of my own babies to sleep.

The love of God is radically particular, enmeshed in the ordinary. Wherever Jesus went, people knew themselves seen and beloved. You see it everywhere throughout the Gospels: Jesus stopping to visit, to name, to recognize, to heal. Children whom nobody else prized, women with wounded bodies or deep spiritual hunger, lepers, soldiers, little ones. He insisted upon it, for these individual souls were those he came to love. He loved the whole world, and that meant each of us in our foibles and fears. I have always cherished the story of when the woman with a disease of bleeding touched him in a crowd and he stopped to ask who, out of hundreds, it might be. I don't think it had a thing to do with anything other than his deep desire for her not to escape without meeting the eyes of the one who loved her wholly, whose gaze could heal what was as twisted and grieved in her soul as it was in her body.

If we could choose to see each other with the intensity and intimate particularity of Christ, we might begin to witness our own love breaking into the darkness of those around us. If we could look at the lives within our reach, quick to spy the needs of all kinds that lurk in wait for the generosity of God's affection, we might understand the power that dwells with us, waiting only upon our offered affection. If we could offer ourselves to meet just the ordinary wounds and financial needs and tiny distresses of those right near us with the radical love of God, we might indeed witness the kingdom come and the blossoming of heaven in our midst.

———

Once a year, amidst the reflective days of Holy Week, I watch a film called *Of Gods and Men*. I watch it in that season because it images to me how love, enduring and unafraid, can sit itself down right in the face of death and defy it with a beauty it cannot comprehend or touch.

The film is based upon the true story of a French Trappist monastery in Algeria where seven monks were kidnapped and killed by Islamic extremists in the '90s. The focus of the story, though, is not upon the death of the monks but on their curious choice to remain in place when confronted with news of their danger. In the film, each monk must wrestle with what his vocation means in the face of death and what it means to remain in love. There is the deep consideration of local friendship and need, for over the years the surrounding villages have become dependent upon the monks for health care and food. But there is also the larger question of their faith: Should the brothers abandon the place in which they have vowed to remain in prayer and ministry simply because they are in danger? What does it mean to love your neighbor when your own life is at risk?

The tension is palpable throughout the film as the brothers debate the decision amongst themselves and carry the mood and weight of it with them in their work. Some see staying as foolish. Why die to make a grand gesture? Some ache at the thought of leaving the people, now friends, to whom they have given their lives in practical service. Some yearn to escape and be free. Some, like the abbot, see the choice to remain as the necessary outflow of their faith, one founded upon a suffering God who endured the violence of the world to reveal God's love.

Interwoven with the scenes of anxious uncertainty within the monastery, and the ones of violence at work outside of it, are interludes showing simply the monks at prayer, in the silence and light of their chapel. You watch them come together, out of their individual desire, into the discipline of fellowship and prayer that is the heart of their shared life. From the individual cacophony of their disagreement, they are drawn into the harmony of the chanted psalms, the call and response of the collects, the Scriptures that make a single unit of them all together, there in the shadow and sweetness of their worship.

To this unity they are drawn, and these scenes foreshadow the decision they reach, for they choose to remain, to be true to their vows of loyalty to person, community, and place. To abide in the place they have vowed to make a refuge of prayer and service to the end of their lives. To keep the vows they have made to each other, as brothers. To keep faith with their neighbors. To stay because love asks them to embody the peacemaking love of Christ that makes a family of all humanity, to witness by the risk and quiet of their presence to a love that cannot be dismayed by any threat the world has to offer. Having reached this resolve, they can welcome both the villagers and the soldiers into their gates for healing. They can carry on with the work they do to relieve the poor. They can plant gardens and bake bread. And they can share what becomes their final feast.

The scene of their festal meal sets an ache in the heart that views it; the camera lingers on each precious face and all-too-vulnerable body around that table, these disparate souls woven back together by their radical choice to face down death with a love that will not falter. Their laughter that night is rich, their fellowship unbroken, as they share a simple meal that is, by virtue of their defiant joy, a feast. They have so completely chosen to remain in love that fear has died away.

And every year I watch it, I pray, *Lord, let love dwell so richly in me that death is ashamed in its presence, as it was in yours upon the cross.*

The great thing in *Of Gods and Men* isn't really the fact of the monks' courage, it's their final recognition that death no longer has the right to define their relationships or actions. Love asks them to remain—with the people they serve, with the place they've chosen, with each other—and in choosing that, they become a fellowship in which the hungry of the world can "touch" real love, as Thomas touched the wounded side of Christ.

When God, in his beauty, reaches into our darkness and grips us with the hand of affection, it's not to individualism that we're summoned. The grip of Beauty is always one of "filiation": by it we are set within the family of God once more, woven back into the story of God's people, empowered to reach and draw the lonely into belonging alongside us. Such a love defies death by becoming the living image of its opposite: of life as it burgeons, leaping from one kindled heart to another.

9

Image

Listening for the Lark

The consolation of fairy-stories, the joy of the happy ending
. . . is a sudden and miraculous grace: never to be counted on
to recur. It does not deny the existence of dyscatastrophe, of
sorrow and failure: the possibility of these is necessary to the
joy of deliverance; it denies (in the face of much evidence, if
you will) universal final defeat and in so far is evangelium, giving a fleeting glimpse of Joy, Joy beyond the walls of the world,
poignant as grief.

> J. R. R. Tolkien, "On Fairy-Stories," in *Tree and Leaf*

The quiet was high and chill in the corridors of the Art Institute
of Chicago as I walked the mazed galleries with coat pulled
close. I walked too swiftly, aware of the restless, unsatisfied dart
of my eyes from painting to gorgeous Impressionist painting.
My looking was too fast, too hungry to drink deeply of their

loveliness; I wanted to pull something from their beauty to answer the need that burned in me. Worn in body and weary in mind, I glanced out the window between the galleries and saw the dirty snow of late winter. I'd traveled for weeks with my parents, working at their conference events, but the travel season with all its pomp and bustle, its distraction from the larger loneliness of my life, was drawing to a close and the long months ahead opened before me like the sere plains of an open desert.

For most of my twenties, I lived in a kind of limbo between my hunger for the life I could imagine—my dreams of education and friendship, of travel and work—and the profound disability of my illness. I always got to the threshold of my dreams. I applied to my favorite universities, planned moves to great cities, tried for different jobs. But I was always hijacked in the final stages by this mental illness whose reach no one in my life fully understood. I was so introverted I did not know how to describe the break with reality that happened for me each time I left home. I didn't know how to articulate the way that the same mind conjuring such a wild loveliness of ambition and creativity could also turn on me, threatening me with so much disaster that I stepped back from the very things I yearned for the most. So I stayed home and worked for my parents and there was goodness in it, but also an increasing and profound sense of failure. I didn't know, because I didn't then understand, how my sense of self was shriveling in the face of this limbo so that I could not see myself as whole or desirable. I didn't know that I increasingly met the world expecting its rejection, and this set a bitter edge to my dreams.

So when I wandered the art museum that day, my sight and senses were those of a caged creature no longer sure that escape was possible. The vivid paintings I usually loved for the

possibility they kindled in my imagination, the countless different lives their beauty suggested I might lead, met me that day as
a subtle taunt: this laughter, this feasting, this companionship
or romance, this writer's autonomy are things you will never
find. So I put my head down and wandered the weathered wood
floors without looking up. I didn't want anyone to see me cry. I
didn't want, again, to be weak. For a while, until the ache in my
throat eased enough for the tears to draw back, I just walked
with face turned away from every beautiful thing.

Until I looked up and beheld a painting whose figure confronted me, accosted me, gripped my gaze in her simplicity and
would not let me turn away. I saw her from across the gallery, a
peasant girl with a scythe in hand, barefoot in a stubbly field,
her clothes rough and wrinkled, her head covered with an old
scarf against the hours of hard work ahead of her. A red sun
grew on the horizon, and this was the only concession to artistic
flourish the artist made, because the painting was profoundly
one of a bleak, exhausting day's work about to begin.

Except it wasn't, because of the girl's uplifted face.

She stood arrested, mouth just a little open, her eyes lifted to
some point beyond the painting's edge. I could feel the sudden
stillness, the way she stopped, surprised, to listen. I could feel
the concentration of her attention upon this one thing. And
the gentle surprise of her wonder, a lovely and irresistible thing
that transformed her. I couldn't look away from that quiet,
receptive face, but I also felt the need to look about me, to find
the same thing that brought such a hushed peace to the whole
of her body.

I glanced at the title of the painting: *The Song of the Lark*
by Jules Breton. As my eyes returned to hers, in that instant,
it was as if the song of that little bird, caroling the coming of

another blessed dawn, echoed through the cold air of that gallery and the desert air of my inmost being. The world stretched stubbly and brown and bleak around us both, but there was this song at play in the open air of the sky. And the joy of it, the high beauty of this daybreak bird singing the world alive, was a power whose loveliness could not be refused.

For a while, I sheltered in the world of that image. I dwelt there in imagination. When I left the museum, it was with a postcard of the painting, and in the days that followed I kept it in my journal, aware of the strange regenerative power of its beauty. During that season, as I dwelt in the calm of that image, I was given the capacity to believe that such a song might break in upon the brown landscape of my own bleak days. My encounter with that painting, so sudden and tiny an event, instigated a shift in the pattern of my thoughts. That image of a weary girl standing in a brown and broken landscape, yet transfigured by some great beauty, spoke to me viscerally of my own capacity to look up and be transformed. The horizons of my closed world opened up. When I stood in the light of that painting, the red sun of that dawn, I could glimpse the in-breaking beauty of love, the presence that haunts the back of each minute, however grieved, and makes it a way forward instead of a dead end. A presence not dependent upon my capacity or effort, but there, waiting to take my weary eyes and lift them up to where the sky grows bright with the dawn.

That moment of rekindled hope was the first of many such gifts in the long, dark years of my illness—a hope specifically mediated to me through works of great artistry. Poems or paintings, music, film, they came to me in unexpected moments, exotic visitors showing up on the doorstep of my heart with an image, a note, a haunting lyric that cut through the shadows binding me. The longer I walked the road of my illness, the more aware I became of the powerful way that great art could grip my hand and lead me forward. There's a kindling power in the light of something created out of a broken human heart, a tenacious creativity that splotches the darkness with gaudy stars and fills the shadows with a siren music of hope and kindles a story like a campfire in our hearts, where we may find refuge and warm our hands.

> I've lived through many ages. I've seen suffering in the darkness. Yet I have seen beauty thrive in the most fragile of places. I have seen the book. The book that turned darkness into light.[1]

When faced with darkness, we have two choices—brilliantly set before us in the little film containing the lines above: we can build a wall or we can make something beautiful. *The Secret of Kells*, a splendid animated story, explores the legend surrounding The Book of Kells, one of the world's most beautiful illuminated manuscripts. The film, with animation drawing on medieval illumination, is an exploration by story and image of what it means to stave off darkness, to keep hold of redemption. The abbot of Kells, a grim man who knows his abbey will inevitably be attacked by Viking raiders, cannot rest until he has built a wall to keep the evil out, and he struggles to see worth in any other endeavor. But Brendan, his nephew, and the delightful illuminator Aidan believe that in the face of evil, the great defiance is to create something so beautiful that it rebukes and transforms the darkness.

For the power in beauty is not brute strength but in the greater vision it offers, a vision to transform and redeem our suffering.

The film draws on what I think earlier generations of Christians understood so much better than we do in the modern world: that art and story, image and song are powerful agents of vision, revealing the life of Christ, resisting the evil of a broken world. The ancients and medievals believed that the whole world was a book, illuminating the mind and imagination of God. When they walked amidst storm and tree, great sky and mighty ocean, they understood themselves as beholding deep and true things about the Word through whom the world came into being, the same Word that took flesh in order to save us. They embodied their own knowledge of salvation in works of art that filled church and home. For centuries, Christian churches were rich in images that told the story of Christ in the crafted beauty depicting his invasion of the darkness. Image and symbol, story and song surrounded worshipers in the catacombs and churches for centuries.

When I was in Florence just before the birth of my daughter, I visited the Convent of San Marco and ambled room to room, delighted by the great works of art by Fra Angelico and others depicting Christ's life but also at the way those images surrounded the monks whether they ate or prayed, worked or slept. They could not escape the story that shaped their lives, the image and drama of it, the vivid color of hope tingeing the air in each room. The monks' cells especially startled me, each with a tiny painting to aid devotion. I nearly laughed aloud when I found one little painting depicting Christ breaking down the door of hell, marching in to save the captive souls, with a demon splayed beneath the shattered door. The humor and pathos of it: to have that image in mind as you struggled with sin or when fear threatened your faith. What power it would offer.

Richard Viladesau, a philosopher and theologian who thought deeply about the role that the arts play in forming our spiritual lives, said that great works of art communicate with us in a way that is "nonverbal, but . . . not for that reason pre-rational or pre-spiritual."[2] Art can actually be "a way of thinking" theologically in and of itself, allowing us a qualitatively different understanding of the world. Jeremy Begbie says that "the arts give expression to a metaphorical way of perceiving the world . . . which reminds us there is always more to the world than we can name, control, and grasp."[3] Oh, surely this is what we need in the midst of our sorrow, the knowledge that something much larger than the broken world has begun, and will end, the story of our lives.

That's what I needed, and it's what *The Lord of the Rings* series supplied.

I like to say that Tolkien saved my faith because, in a way, he did. In those years when I could barely read Scripture, when beauty was the last thing I found in the Bible, I oddly devoured the whole of Tolkien's mythology. I think God must have chuckled. I discovered it when I was seventeen and spent hours in those first months of searing obsessions sitting on my bed with a massive, battered copy of the trilogy in my lap. I lived and breathed that story because in it I found a world that reflected the drama and yearning, the shattering evil and luminous beauty that vied for supremacy in my heart. I found figures of courage who defied the darkness, souls who wrought hidden kingdoms of undying beauty by way of brave resistance. That book translated the bleak new landscape of my suffering into a world that I could navigate by story and tenuous hope.

One day, I sat on my bed, wishing with the whole of my being that Middle Earth was real and that there were such places as

Rivendell where I could take shelter. I thought perhaps I too could be brave in that world, I too could believe in Sam's "light and high beauty beyond the touch of darkness."[4] If only such a world were true. But a sly, sweet whisper blew through my brain: if Tolkien created Middle Earth, and the whole of his imagination was only the briefest refraction of God's mind, then God's real story must be one of such engrossing radiance, such true battle and world-changing courage, that Tolkien himself could barely imagine it. And if this story was the true story of the world, if my life and my illness were the stuff of God's epic, then the courage imaged in Tolkien's story wasn't something to dream about, it was something for which I, in the *real* world, must quest. I spent whole months in those years reading Tolkien, then the Bible, letting the story offered by one struggling, faithful author renew my capacity to see God's beauty in his Word and at work in his world.

"The value of the myth," said C. S. Lewis in *On Stories*, "is that it takes all the things we know and restores to them the rich significance which has been hidden by 'the veil of familiarity.' . . . By putting bread, gold, horse, apple, or the very roads into a myth, we do not retreat from reality: we rediscover it."[5]

Lewis was a comrade in arms with Tolkien when it came to their shared belief in the power of artistry and imagination to gesture to the full splendor of God's reality. Lewis, before his conversion, read George MacDonald's *Phantastes* and said it "baptized" his imagination. But even the Norse myths he passionately loved allowed him a glimpse of divine love, for the whole of his being was stirred by the lyric describing the death of a god, "Balder the beautiful is dead," and years later he would recognize that it was Christ he glimpsed in that fragment of ancient story.

Lewis and Tolkien were two of a fellowship, The Inklings, writers who all understood that there are different ways of knowing: that imagination allows us the inside, experiential knowledge we taste within a story as we encounter the world created within our imaginations. In an age decimated by war and loss, they recognized that such an encounter with beauty, an "inside" experience of imagination such as they had each found in a story, might be the only way that some in the postwar world could regain any hold on healing or hope. Tolkien argued for this with particular power: born, I think, from the darkness and grief he knew in the trenches of the First World War. His essay "On Fairy-Stories" defended the power of imaginative stories to allow us to both glimpse and desire redemption. He described the famous "happy ending" of fairy tales as "eucatastrophe . . . a sudden and miraculous grace; never to be counted on to recur. It does not deny the existence of dyscatastrophe, of sorrow and failure. . . . It denies (in the face of much evidence if you will) universal final defeat and in so far is evangelium, giving a fleeting glimpse of Joy, Joy beyond the walls of the world, poignant as grief."[6]

Tolkien's luminous claim is that fairy stories allow us to actually taste real joy, the kind rooted in Christ, which will mend and make right our sorrow and which is a grace that comes to us from outside the realm of time. In using the term *evangelium*, Tolkien makes clear his belief that the "consolation" of faerie stories ultimately images the resurrection of Christ and the glory of a world remade by Love. "Joy beyond the walls of the world": this is the gift of fairy tales, but also of great works of art and music and poetry. This is the "Joy" C. S. Lewis knew as a boy, one that drew him finally to belief in God because it worked in him as "an unsatisfied desire which itself was more desirable than any other satisfaction."[7]

Owen Barfield, friend to both Tolkien and Lewis, described the effect of poetry upon us as "a felt change of conscious-ness,"[8] and this is the sense of renewed insight that I think at-tends every piece of art that kindles our vision. When sorrow has made us incapable of imagining a good future, when grief has diminished our world—oh then, art, music, film, and story break in upon us as agents of rescue, cutting our imaginations free from despair, helping us to our feet where we can see out the window of our minds into the far lands of hope once more. As Andrew Davison writes in *Imaginative Apologetics*, "Literature can come to us as a holy invitation to 'taste and see' what it is like to live and think in the light of God's goodness."[9] A novel can offer someone mired in the closed horizons of suffering the possibility of seeing the world in the light of God's intimate presence within their pain.

But once that beauty has come to us, what does it require of *us*?

Beauty calls us to create. Before the breaking of the world, we were formed in the image of an artist God whose first acts in time were those of profound and beautiful creation. To be made in his image and redeemed by his love is, inescapably, to be called to creation. To craft and form, to fill or beautify, these are labors not only of artists, but of those remade by Love, part-nered with their Creator in the healing of the world. Madeleine L'Engle, one of my beloved writers, wrote that "unless we are creators we are not fully alive," for "creativity is a way of life."[10]

What does this mean for us, the sorrowing and the healed, the aching and redeemed?

———

I did not know what to create and thought the world wouldn't want what I could offer if I did. Throughout my twenties, I typed away at poems stretched and aching with emotion, with half-baked stories that couldn't bear the burden of all I wanted them to say. I kept them in files on my laptop, never quite ready to show them to anyone else, uncertain of their worth. I listened to and far too often believed the voice of my illness when it told me that anything I created would be marred, incapable of communicating the deep things I understood about beauty or hope. *You are broken*, went the whispers as I wrote, *and what you make will be too*. For I had not yet fully understood that pain is an agent of diminishment, lessening us in our own eyes, and this too is one of the griefs that Beauty comes to heal by calling us to do precisely what we have begun to believe we can't.

One day, late in my twenties, I came to try again at writing in a little downtown shop where books lined the walls and the air hummed with slow, jazzy music. I managed very little the first hour and soon heaved a sigh. I cupped my coffee close, sipped it slow, and let my sleepy eyes roam over the rim of the mug. I began to spy on a girl at the table next to mine. A scholarly air hovered about her along with heaps of textbooks, stacked notebooks, and four different kinds of pens. She was clearly working very hard: eyes down under her fringe of dark hair, pen at a swift scratch, earbuds wedged in tight against the lazy aura of the place.

But every so often she stopped, and this was what gripped my attention. With a distinct sigh, she reached for her mocha and set down her pen. And as she sipped, she stared. For propped against the nearest pile of books was a vivid photo of Audrey Hepburn. My neighbor fixed her eyes on that photo, never blinking as she took a long sip of coffee and chocolate. Then she set down her mug, wriggled up a little straighter in her seat, and set to work again. I couldn't help my surreptitious stare.

The strength she obviously took from that photo fascinated me, as if in fixing her eyes upon it she received some new shock of courage.

I turned reluctantly back to my own book-piled table and cappuccino. A blank computer screen and blank notebook were open before me. I ignored them and opened the topmost book on my pile, a series of essays by the poet Denise Levertov. I was only one paragraph in before I stopped, eyes arrested by these words:

> I believe poets are . . . makers, craftsmen: it is given to the seer to see, but it is then his responsibility to communicate what he sees, that they who cannot see may see, since we are "members one of another."[11]

I had studied many facets of the writer's vocation, but this idea of Levertov's startled and stung me. She seemed to class faithfulness in creativity with spiritual imperatives like loving your neighbor and telling no lies. I squirmed in my seat, abruptly uneasy in conscience. I knew that I had seen a little in the way she had described, for beauty had come to me so often in my sorrow. I knew that worlds waited to be created within me: the scenes and people that brimmed my imagination, the joy glimpsed like light on a far-off hilltop, the story worlds that come to my mind more as gift than anything else. But rarely did I share them, and I'd never thought of sharing my writing as one aspect of my obedience to God's healing presence in my life.

Writing terrified me; it always had. Not the easy kind of freelance work and editing projects and countless small jobs. Those I could accomplish with mind alone—thankful to earn my bread and grateful, I admit, to avoid those clamorous dreams that beg to be told. Because oh, I didn't know how to begin to set the best things forth. I half began, then drew back in fear. My imagination blazed with pictures begging to be written, but my words seemed too frail to bear them. I'd set down countless sentences, cast dozens of hours to typing away, only to scrap the whole thing in sheer frustration. The truth was that I did not think I could do my story justice. I doubted my skill. I doubted my vision. I wondered if the worlds I know within myself might be deemed just silly by a reader, and I didn't want to be mocked. So the stories stayed locked in the little room of my head and fear was the bolt on its door.

I glanced again at the girl next to me to escape the discomfort now burning in my throat and I wondered, *What does she "see," what true vision does she touch through her contemplation of Audrey Hepburn? Did Audrey know she was embodying an ideal, and did she offer it willingly?* I glanced down at my own table, and my eyes wandered to the pile of books I toted with me. And again, my heart burned with conviction. For each of the books before me had been the sort of gift that Levertov described, stories that allowed me to see, to taste, to grope my way forward when I felt blind. I would not have defied certain moments of darkness, would not have known how to hope, without the vision provided to me by a few generous writers.

I opened their stories in the evenings, when my heart and mind were exhausted with the overthinking required by major decisions and the fear that always laced them for me. The worlds they had made and the people they presented were a refuge to me. Wendell Berry's Port William. The Eliot family and their home of Damerosehay in Elizabeth Goudge's *Pilgrim's Inn*. The artistic grit of Thea in Willa Cather's *Song of the Lark*. Nouwen's story of God's mercy in his *The Return of the Prodigal Son*, traced through his contemplations on Rembrandt's painting of the prodigal returned.

They sheltered me. When I was blinded by doubt, I journeyed on by the vibrant light of their created worlds. As I struggled toward wisdom, feeling homeless in soul as I teetered between my hope and my fear, those stories took my tired hands and tugged me forward. I was nourished by the power of what they presented as possible. I caught my breath again as I sojourned within their scenes, walked beside their characters, then stood back on my own two feet to reclaim my own vision and walk the long road required to bring it to life.

As I mulled this, I pulled out my journal and paged back through my last months of notes, skimming the quotations I'd jotted down from those companion books. At one particularly long quotation, I stopped, reading again a favorite passage from Cather's *Song of the Lark*. In it, the heroine Thea, like me, feels battered by the wide world in which she is fighting to establish her own vision of life. But Dvořák's *New World Symphony* revives and steels her for the challenge. I read the scene again, which described how she walked out of a concert with a fierce resolve born from the sheer power of the beautiful music:

A cloud of dust blew in her face and blinded her. There was some power abroad in the world bent upon taking away from her that feeling with which she had come out of the conference hall. Everything seemed to sweep down on her to tear it out from under her cape. . . . Thea glared round her at the crowds, the ugly, sprawling streets, the long lines of lights, and she was not crying now. . . . Very well; they should never have it. As long as she lived that ecstasy was going to be hers. She would live for it, work for it, die for it; but she was going to have it, time after time, height after height. She could hear the crash of the orchestra again, and she rose on the brasses. She would have it, what the trumpets were singing![12]

And just like the girl at the table next to me, I sat suddenly straighter in my seat. There I was, reading about another person sheltered in trial by the vision offered by an artist. Dvořák's music sheltered Thea (and no doubt Cather, Thea's creator) when she doubted and renewed her strength to fight—to acknowledge the beauty she knew as the real thing over against the clamor of the world. I flipped the page of my journal. There, in like manner, were Nouwen's words about Rembrandt's painting of the prodigal son, telling how the color, line, and form so faithfully painted by one man ushered him into the arms of the Father's mercy. Rembrandt's vision sheltered Nouwen. And that encounter produced Nouwen's book, whose vision now sheltered me. And suddenly I was breathless.

Every work of art reaches out across the centuries, and each is a vision that casts a flame into the darkness. The wonder is that one great light wakes another. The song of one wakens the story of another. The story she told became the poem he made that kindled the painting in yet another's hands. Each is a work of obedience. No artist can cast their flame of vision without a twinge of fear that it will simply fade or even pass unseen. But each is also a work of generosity: precious, private worlds offered in a self-forgetfulness that pushes aside vanity, insecurity, and perfectionistic pride.

Levertov is right. The visions set forth in the books (and paintings and songs) we turn to for hope are offerings of love, given in the recognition that we truly are members of one another. We all bear the same hunger for eternity. We all walk forward in the dark of doubt, reaching for something we can't quite name. We all walk blind and grieved in our suffering. We yearn to discover who we are meant to become, what it is we hunger to find in those midnight hours when our hearts will not be sated. But the artists and storytellers and makers of song offer the inner vision they have known as a sign of hope to the hungering world. They invite us into the sacred, inmost rooms of their minds and let us stand at the windows of their own imaginations where we glimpse, ah, wonders we might never have dreamed alone.

Madeleine L'Engle, in contemplating what it means to be a Christian and a creator, said this:

> I believe that each work of art, whether it is a work of great genius, or something very small, comes to the artist and says, "Here I am. Enflesh me. Give birth to me." And the artist either says, "My soul doth magnify the Lord," and willingly becomes the bearer of the work, or refuses.[13]

Beauty bears God's life to us, but it always calls us, in turn, to bear the life of God to the rest of the broken world. The goodness we have known always places the gentle demand of love upon us, that we witness to its reality and offer it in our turn as healing to our neighbor. Some of the greatest works of art in the world have come from the obedience of suffering souls to speak the truest things they found in their pain. Frederick Buechner, whose own luminous books were born from his deep grief, wrote a book called *Speak What We Feel: Not What We Ought to Say*, a title drawn from the tragic lines in Shakespeare's *King Lear*. Exploring the poetry of Gerard Manley Hopkins, the novels of Mark Twain and G. K. Chesterton, and the plays of Shakespeare, he considered how the masterpieces of each were born out of their deep suffering and their wrestle toward hope. In doing so, he shows us what we too may bring forth from the heart of our own darkness.

That day in the cafe, I glanced again at the girl next to me as these understandings suffused my brain. She was unrelentingly diligent. Who knew what she was writing, perhaps in response to the beauty she knew? I brushed my hand over the books whose weathered covers bore the scuff and dent of my many readings. The life within them crackled under my hand. I met the stare of my own silent notebook, blank before me, and my pen sitting lonely on the page. I sighed and wriggled up a little straighter in my chair. I picked up that pen. At the very least, I knew I could write what I had just seen and understood.

And that is where art, and hope, begin.

10

Saint

A Hidden Life

There is only one tragedy in the end: Not to have been a saint.

Charles Péguy

In the book of Job, that great drama aching with all the questions and arguments of suffering, one of Job's friends asks what he thinks is an obvious question: "If you are righteous, what do you give to Him [God]?" (Job 35:7 NASB). The friend meant this to put Job in his place, for of course he assumed that Job ought to know that we can "give" nothing to the God who is the Maker of us and everything we see. But in the drama of Job, the question is profoundly revealing: the whole book of Job is shaped by the idea that Job actually does offer something to God by his continuing righteousness in the face of his pain. His faithfulness, his fierce refusal to curse God, though he does not know it then, is a mighty and devastating answer to the Satan figure in the story, who taunted God with the claim that no one is righteous for nothing.

For that was the assumption of the ancient world in which Job lived. Worship and blessing were a tit-for-tat exchange in all the religions of the ancient Near East. If you did what the gods told you, then your life would be blessed. Defy them, and you suffered. Suffering was seen as the consequence simply of improper behavior, and this was assumed even by the followers of Yahweh, the one God who entered into covenant relationship with his people. The story of Job, then, was subversive—a drama meant to challenge and upend all the assumptions of religion, as Robert Frost's poem puts it:

> Stultify the Deuteronomist
> and change the tenor of religious thought.[1]

Job and God together are suddenly catapulted into a new and wild landscape. They must encounter each other anew, driven by a question asked in heaven that must be answered on earth even though it can never be revealed. Job has to renegotiate the terms of his faith and the depth of his devotion. With all his visible blessings removed, with all evidence of God's love stripped away, he has to decide whether he will continue to fear God, not for what God gives him, but for who he truly believes God to be. Job's heart becomes the ground where the faith of Israel is challenged to mature into something far more beautiful than the tit-for-tat righteousness of the pagan world. Job, wrestling with both fidelity and grief, becomes the model for new worshipers, the kind of people God makes us in Christ: not merely servants who believe as long as they're paid but children who love because they trust that their Father is good.

I've thought often of Job in the midst of my OCD, for I too have deeply sensed that my pain was the space in which I was invited to a faith far deeper and sweeter than any I had yet known. Not because God willed my pain or needed it to make me mature. Not because it was necessary or required. But because I had the chance to engage with the radical goodness of God, a force so real in the lives of those who love him that it can take the very devastation that Satan intended to be the destruction and end of faith and transform it into a life irradiated by the kind of love that cannot be broken by darkness.

My suffering is where I have most keenly understood what it means to be called a *saint*.

That word: we hear it as the exception to workaday humanity. We hear it as an extreme state to be reached only by effort or grit or some given thing we haven't yet figured out how to offer. Yet this is the identity to which we who love God and wrestle to know him in a fallen world are called, and I believe our suffering is often the space where we actually discover this fact. Our brokenness marks the moment our resources fail. But sainthood was never a matter of our great strength. Sainthood grows, like a baby hidden in the womb, in the space we make for God's goodness to fill and transform our darkness; it begins when we refuse, Job-like, to curse God, and instead prepare for his arrival amidst our anguish. Sainthood is the simple process by which the life of God so illumines and fills the empty places of our sorrowing hearts that we are filled up brimful with him: his goodness directing our actions, forming our words, quieting our anguish, driving our compassion until we begin to resemble the whole and healed creations we will fully become in the new world ahead.

And that is a beauty more potent than any other the world has known.

But often, it's a hidden glory.

It's a beauty that doesn't play on the stage of society or across our social media platforms or in the garish headlines. Sainthood is so often a thing of quiet souls at faithful work in difficult, ordinary lives. George Eliot, great novelist of the human condition, closed one of her most famous stories with these lines:

> The growing good of the world is partly dependent on unhistoric acts; and that things are not so ill with you and me as they might have been, is half owing to the number who lived faithfully a hidden life.[2]

My illness set me in a hidden life, and for a while I was convinced that because of that I'd never be able to do anything great for God. I could barely leave home. I second-guessed every decision. My health was uncertain. I was prone to panic attacks and insecurity, unable even to express my own opinions in social situations because of a crippling self-consciousness. I dreamed of being a professor at a great university, or caring for orphans in a war zone, or writing the kind of novel that would shift the hearts of a generation. But my life was a round of mundanity: quiet times in the morning, local work or writing when I could, meals with my family, evening walks, nights at home. Stuff so achingly ordinary, so void, I thought, of anything to offer so mighty a God.

Until I realized that he calls himself "lowly and meek," and that the hidden minutes of my ordinary were the only thing he ever wanted to begin with . . .

———————

I've known saints of hidden lives.

Souls grown great in their luminous and quiet fidelity to make God welcome in the dark and silent spaces of their journey.

One in particular changed my life. She was my mother's best friend before I was even a sparkle in my parents' eyes. My "tante" is one of the figures whose shape glimmers in the background of my earliest memories, the impressionist ones from the years when my parents lived in Vienna. She was exotic to me, visiting us from Austria each Christmas, bringing a bevy of small, wrapped presents enclosing tiny treasures gathered for me in her travels. She arrived with the chill spice of winter and the golden excitement of the holidays, wearing lovely Austrian coats and a faint perfume, her laugh deep and throaty. She was sophisticated, and her life in Vienna among diplomats and missionaries, amidst all the loveliness of the city, was an image of what I hoped I would one day find.

But the same year we moved to Tennessee, the same year that I turned eighteen and watched the horizons of my possibilities close in the face of my mental illness, she moved back home to Kentucky where her mother was in decline with Alzheimer's. Just like that, the whole of her lovely life changed and she moved from the music-haunted streets of Vienna back to the tiny, rather forgotten little town where she had grown up—to the cottage of her childhood with the brown braided rugs and the old kitchen table in a weathered bay window and a mother whose memory was unraveling by the day.

Watching her do it, I wondered if she resented the loss of her beautiful Viennese life. She visited us often those first months in Tennessee and soon had invited me to stay. Gwen's house felt safe, and my mom—desperate, I'm sure, for me to have some outlet beyond our home—encouraged me to drive up for an overnight or two at a time. So I did. I loved Gwen and wanted to get to know her for myself, and I knew quite well that she was the most creative and delightful of hostesses. I expected good meals and company. But I'm not sure I expected anything more. Since I so deeply resented the limitations imposed upon me by illness, I think I assumed on some level that she must feel the same way, caught as she was in the country, cut off from the rich city life of art and music, with an increasingly disabled elderly mother who would need intensive and demanding care. Though I never actually spoke the words, I assumed she must be disappointed—for how could such a loss of freedom, such a limiting of scope, be anything but a diminishment of richness, a lessening of joy?

But *diminishment* is not a word Gwen ever met.

And what she invited me into was not a life made less by limitations but one whose spaces were so thoroughly and richly cultivated by love that whole worlds grew up in the rooms of her little home. She named the cottage Eben Haus, the "eben" a reference to the Hebrew word meaning "stone of help." That name was her claiming, I think, of that space as the place where God would come in the fullness of his grace. It was no easy thing to do, for Gwen had already lost both her brothers and her father, and that house must have echoed with the memory of people loved . . . and taken by death.

But it was not death I tasted there. Over the two years of my weekly visits, and about ten more years of longer sojourns in autumn and spring, what I knew was something I can only describe as God's own life, so radiant and delicious that I would not dare to call it anything less than full.

Gwen made more of an ordinary day than most people do of a week. When I was at Eben Haus, I was caught up in a way of living that saw each square of the ordinary as a space made for the crafting of joy. In all my visits, we never finished everything we set ourselves to do; there were simply too many good things to accomplish. We cooked prodigiously; she insisted that I do small things well, that I learn the skill of a well-turned pie crust and the discipline of frugality in which no scrap of food is left to waste. She taught me the pleasure of taking the spaces we have (not the ones we wish we had) and making them beautiful, for room by room she made that little old house the work of her artistry. I watched her design a stained-glass window and save for it for weeks. And plan a room of built-in bookshelves and oversee their building for months.

Our days had a rich rhythm that varied only with our choice of which good things we'd try. We always opened our mornings with coffee and talk and the sharing of Scripture or a choice bit of poem. We cooked: coconut pie and chicken dumplings, creamed corn and sourdough bread. We gardened: I learned to trim roses and hydrangeas, to hunt with her for plants at the local Amish nursery. We cleaned the porch furniture where we'd rest each afternoon with Larla (her mother) and settled there after the task with cups of tea and books. We spread out our Bibles at the kitchen table and studied until it was time to start dinner. She took me with her to visit her neighbors and friends and made me a guest at her many small gatherings.

The care she gave her mama was a thing that awed me. In a world where most people as old and needy as Larla would be sent to a nursing home, Gwen kept her mother in the room she had always known so that as her memory went she'd still have the things she knew by rote around her. As she grew feeble, Gwen took on the work of feeding and dressing her alone. Of speaking her back into a sense of belonging when Larla did not recognize even her daughter. I can only guess at how deeply the slow, sure loss of her mother must have hurt Gwen, how much it must have cost her to watch it, to be the one who walked with her to the closing of death, yet it was also a space of profound beauty. I think Gwen must have opened the care of her mother, the cost and grief of it, so fully to God that it became a space of radiant love. To see Gwen pat her mama's hand, help her to bed, serve her toast and eggs, or tell her all the sweet things she'd forgotten made one of the truest images of God's love I've ever known.

Sometimes in the afternoon we took Larla on long drives through the countryside with our favorite Celtic music as soundtrack. We watched the leaves turn in autumn and the forsythias bloom in spring, and with Gwen, I learned the names of local things and the value of loving the square of earth one is given, wherever it is. One day, we visited the graves of her family and I watched her eyes sweep the gentle green swell of the hills, the stretch of the old trees, her gaze deep with peace.

"I guess this is beauty enough for me," she said.

And I think that was the orientation of her heart, to open herself so wholly to receive the goodness of God in whatever place she found herself that there was no such thing as limitation or lack. There was just her willing heart, sated by the beauty God gave. I know there must have been darkness— moments when her burdens must have weighed like lead upon her shoulders—yet those did not define her story.

One particular visit was so perfect and joyous to us both that we felt we had to name it. The trees round Gwen's house had kindled themselves into a gorgeous autumn fire that marked each day with dramatic beauty. Our meals all came out to gourmet perfection. Our drives were unforgettable, our talks deep.

There was a quality of such distilled joy that we decided to call that visit our "halcyon days."

Years later, in writing this book, I returned to this memory and to that strange word, *halcyon*. I knew the term from hours of reading old books, where it's often used to describe a season of peace and happiness. But its origin is strange and lovely. It's from an ancient Greek myth about a woman who threw herself upon the sea when her husband died in a shipwreck. The gods, in pity, transformed both of them into "halcyon" birds, or kingfishers: those gorgeous, swift, sapphire-winged birds of the water. When the wife went to lay her eggs, the winds and waves threatened them, so Aeolus, god of the winds, restrained the storms for seven days. These became known as "halcyon days," when no storms were allowed to roar.

There is a sense in which every day I spent at Eben Haus was a halcyon day, for it was a halcyon space, made safe and calm because it was filled with the peace and goodness of God. And yet, it was a place, in its origin, beset by storms, a space that could have been shaped by the brooding unrest of limitation and disappointment. It became a halcyon space precisely because Gwen, my precious friend, embodied the kind of radiance that is my idea of sainthood, offered the storm-dark spaces of her world to God and let him fill them with a light and beauty that made her one of the people in whose hidden lives the broken world is mended.

Gwen's story made it possible for me to imagine such a story for myself.

I don't think it's any coincidence that Gwen was the one who introduced me to Wendell Berry because she reminds me so much of a character in one of his books.

If you read much of anything I've written or spend more than five minutes in my company, you'll hear me quote some line of Mr. Berry's poems or stories. I'm happy to be called a bit of a Berry fanatic, and I want everyone I know to read him because he taught me something that few modern writers have understood: we are called to fidelity. We are called to faithfulness, to lives whose soil becomes the place where the stories of others are rooted. We are members one of another, and the way we deal with our sorrow and claim our hope will become the soil for the stories of our children and our spouses, our neighbors and our friends.

This is one of the gifts of the quiet sainthood that comes through our suffering.

One of my favorite Berry novels is called *Remembering*, a story of fellowship and fidelity that images just the kind of workaday saint I believe we're all called to be. I read this book first as a frustrated girl trapped in my room by illness and found my whininess scuppered by the book's call to fidelity. I read it again when I took it as a theme for my graduate dissertation and realized that it was a book precisely about that hidden power of sainthood learned in suffering that so interested me.

Andy Catlett, the hero of this brief tale, is a character in many of Berry's books, as every story Mr. Berry writes is set in the fictional town of Port William. Andy had been a boy when I read about him in *Hannah Coulter*, but now he was a man who had made the hard decision to leave a city job and return to the farming and family he had left when he was young. He did it in faith, hoping for roots and belonging. But the story opens in a dark San Francisco hotel room where Andy is questioning not only his decision but everything he loves. Having lost his hand in a freak farming accident, he feels useless, is alienated from his wife, is far from home, has been rejected by his peers, and feels that he is a relic from an old time never to be reclaimed. He is a sort of Job figure whose troubles cut him off from all the goodness he has known.

The first chapters are surreal; as a reader I felt disoriented. Only at the end of the book did I realize that I was meant not just to read but to experience the terror of being unmoored by grief, disoriented by suffering—the very sense I have known in mental illness. Everything becomes strange. Andy wanders the streets, wondering if he can return to the life he thought he had chosen in Kentucky. In his isolation, he is vulnerable to believing what he has told himself for months, that his life and presence are worthless: and this tempts him to faithlessness. Untethered from the obligations of home life—the knowledge, the belonging of those who love him—he walks out into the pre-dawn city and away from his home, his family, and his marriage, imagining a solitary self and a different life, different women, different homes. He is heading for self-destruction, for the breaking of his vows and the loss of his love.

But then there is a moment as dawn creeps up the edge of the ocean. He sits on a bench, watching the sunrise. And he begins to *remember*.

His memory comes in a series of visions, histories passed down through his family that, image by image, restore his capacity to imagine what it means to hope amidst despair, to love even from a place of brokenness. The story of when his grandparents faced ruin at the failure of a crop, and his grandmother scrawled a psalm on a scrap of paper in blind faith: "out of the depths have I cried unto thee, O Lord." Or the coming of his grandfather after the brutal years of the Civil

War to court and marry his grandmother. Or the integrity of Elton, Andy's mentor, who won the respect of those about him with "his straight clear look." Or the work of his grandmother, who lovingly did the chores that "had been done forever."

The visions that come to him are, in their way, simply the history of his own being, family tales that have become embedded in his imagination, stories of the people in whom his own life is rooted. The memories aren't actually his own, yet as stories that speak to his identity they do belong to him, and they reach out to him even as he stands at the edge of destruction. In remembering the people whose lives and work, integrity and fortitude and neighborliness made possible his own, he is jolted out of his thick, hazed dream of despair. In a luminous passage that is the turning point of the book, Andy looks out over the ocean and understands that in his grief

> he is held though he does not hold. . . . He has met again his one life and one death, and taken them back . . . a barn seventy-five feet by forty, a hundred acres of land, six generations of his own history partly failed, and a few dead and living whose love has claimed him forever. He will be partial and he will die, he will live out the truth of that. Though he does not hold, he is held. He is grieving, and he is full of joy.[3]

To remember, for Andy, is to have his vision healed. He recognizes and finally accepts his own frailty, the limits of his own existence, exchanging his bitterness for his renewed vision of his own life as a farmer and husband, a father and neighbor. He must keep faith with "the love that has claimed him." That moment, standing at the edge of the Pacific Ocean, he turns, and every step after is a step toward his home where he will give himself again to the work of faithfulness and love.

But there is one person in particular who has kept faith with Andy through all the days of his bitterness and pain. Flora, Andy's wife, has borne his injustice, his fury, his grief, and his seeming abandonment with the quiet grace of fidelity. She has kept the faith: of farm chores and home life and children comforted. The novel finds its climax in the scene of Andy's homecoming. The house is empty, but Flora, knowing he's on his way, leaves a note saying the family has gone to pick beans. Her quiet welcome, her invitation back into the rich ordinary of their shared life, is his true moment of homecoming. Here he returns not just from his physical journey but from the alienation caused by his grief. His homecoming is of restored vision, one in which he knows himself blessed.

> He is walking now, from room to room in the house where he has hated and struggled so fiercely, he is breathing in the smell of the life that the two of them have made . . . and he is saying over and over to himself, "I am blessed, I am blessed."[4]

Only by the hidden and quiet lives of countless others was Andy able to return to the knowledge of his blessedness. Only in their fidelity, their offering up of grief, their weaving of grace into sorrow was he made capable of choosing the sainthood of suffering for himself.

If there is one great beauty to which we are called by the in-breaking goodness of God, it is this kind of faithfulness. We are called to be Andy, reawakened to our blessedness, but also to be Flora, who keeps that blessedness safe when Andy cannot grasp it. My mother was like Flora; I remember the power of her words in the early days of my illness when I told her I didn't think I could keep believing in God. "That's all right," she said, "I'll believe for you." And she did, holding tenaciously to me in love as I struggled with anger and doubt. She listened to my endless confessions, my countless anxieties, my wild frustration. She held when I could not hold, though I know the anguish it cost her. But my mama, who has suffered deeply herself, understood that as Beauty invades and transforms our suffering, as we are drawn from grief into wonder, we are called to become souls in whose presence the angry and anguished may discover both belonging and restored blessedness. A sainthood of hidden grace that transforms the life of each who encounters it.

It is a sainthood we can live, in the long run, only if we too are remembering. For sainthood, you know, is not about effort but the open-armed receiving of God's healing life. Sainthood is, at heart, a matter of wonder.

At the end of the story of Job, God comes to talk with him, and this is quite the radical turnout of the tale. For Job has spent a whole book vociferously claiming his innocence. He's a garrulous man, bemoaning his existence, wishing for death, and though he never sins or curses God, he does berate God and summon him like a lawyer dog-collaring a witness for a trial. His friends stand by aghast, pretty sure that Job's going to get struck with lightning for his impertinence.

But God breaks all expectations by actually appearing. He shows up just like Job demands, not there to smash Job into oblivion but simply to talk. They have two conversations, and at first, Job doesn't seem too happy with God's reply. For God's "answer" is to ask Job questions he cannot possibly answer. In a mighty poem of a passage, God takes Job on a tour of the universe, challenging Job to consider not only the mystery of his own suffering but the mystery of existence itself as sustained by God's power, upheld by God's presence, rooted in his goodness. But Job seems unimpressed by the grandeur paraded before him. His only confession is that he is "of small account" and "will not answer" again (40:4–5). Considering his vociferous previous passages of question, outrage, and need, this response must be seen mostly as indicating a standoff. It is a bit passive-aggressive, like a child before a bully: I'm smaller than you, leave me alone.

This is where I think Job and God stand at the crossroads of suffering and sainthood. If their conversation ended with the first speech, I think we'd have to view Job closing his heart to God's questions and pleas. But God is not content with Job's response and summons him once more to listen. And the whole story turns as Job engages his heart and opens it to wonder.

In the second half of God's great address to Job, the cadence and flow of God's speech gently shifts from the clip of instruction to the lyrical flow of delight. God yearns for Job to recognize the magnificence of creation and what the beauty of it speaks about its Creator. There is an aching invitation for Job to move out of the closed room of his angry question into the opened horizon of a "worldview that arises from a wondering."[5]

And for whatever reason is hidden in his heart, Job does.

His second answer, as he beholds God's magnificence and accepts it as evidence of a goodness that holds and redeems him in his pain, is profoundly different from his first. He speaks now of marvels "too wonderful for me" (42:3), and his words to God are achingly beautiful. "Hear, and I will speak" (42:4), says Job, whose voluminous complaints, whose outraged sense of justice, whose fierce demands for God's answers have filled whole pages. In a book marked and driven by Job's impossible questions about suffering, Job now makes an assertive and complete statement, ending a drama of questions with his answer to God, "I know" (42:2), and his confession that "I had heard of you by the hearing of the ear, but now my eye sees you" (42:5), an awed and grateful wondering that makes him capable of recognizing God's presence and power at work in the broken world.

This is the moment that Job becomes a saint.

The history of suffering shifts as Job steps into the light of God's presence, as he lifts his face to look upon the God who has arrived in the midst of his suffering with a beauty that cannot be gainsaid and a light that cannot be quenched. That passage—"I have seen," "now I know"—echoes with Andy's shocked realization: I am blessed, I am blessed, I am blessed.

To be a saint begins with the choice to join Job and Andy in their awe.

What do we give God?

Our loving wonder. For with that gift, we make ourselves hospitable to his life, our inmost beings ready to receive his world-renewing goodness. We become like Mary, the woman who bore God into the world by her openhearted yes in the face of mystery and pain. We too find ourselves summoned and startled in the tiny "annunciations" of God's beauty amidst our grief. Denise Levertov's poem "Annunciation" describes them as moments

> when roads of light and storm
> open from darkness in a man or woman.[6]

Let light, then, be the road that winds heavenward from our grieved hearts. Let the story of love run onward into the world from our healed souls. For what evil intended as the end of trust and the death of hope, God made the space of his richest coming. He fills the void of our darkness with the living Word of his radiant self, speaking a world of beauty so rich and gorgeous into our hearts that we may stand in wonder and know ourselves unendingly blessed.

In that wonder, in that sated and saintly blessedness, we ourselves become his living and beautiful truth.

Notes

Chapter 1 This Is the Broken Place

1. Fyodor Dostoevsky, *Idiot* (United Kingdom: Wordsworth Editions Limited, 1996), 365.

2. Augustine of Hippo, https://www.goodreads.com/quotes/669135-late -have-i-loved-you-o-beauty-ever-ancient-ever.

3. Gerard Manley Hopkins, "As Kingfishers Catch Fire," in *Poems* (London: Humphrey Milford, 1918), Bartleby.com, 1999, www.bartleby.com/122/.

Chapter 2 To Wrestle Is Righteous

1. Michael Lloyd, "Are Animals Fallen?," in *Animals on the Agenda: Questions about Animals for Theology and Ethics*, ed. Andrew Linzey and Dorothy Yamamoto (London: SCM Press, 1998), 147–60.

Chapter 3 Beauty Is Truth

1. Alexander Schmemann, *For the Life of the World* (Crestwood, NY: St. Vladimir's Seminary Press, 2004), 14.

2. Elizabeth von Arnim, *The Enchanted April* (Lexington, KY: Seven Treasures, 2009), 73.

3. Von Arnim, *Enchanted April*, 40.

4. Hans Urs von Balthasar, *Seeing the Form*, vol. 1 of *The Glory of the Lord: A Theological Aesthetics,* in Twentieth Century Religious Thought, vol. 1: Christianity (San Francisco: Ignatius Press, 2009), 18.

5. Balthasar, *Seeing the Form*, 18.

6. Balthasar, *Seeing the Form*, 18.

7. David Bentley Hart, *The Doors of the Sea* (Grand Rapids: Eerdmans, 2011), 60.

8. Schmemann, *For the Life of the World*, 19.

9. Schmemann, *For the Life of the World*, 15.

10. Schmemann, *For the Life of the World*, 20.

11. Edna St. Vincent Millay, "God's World," in *Modern American Poetry*, ed. Louis Untermeyer (New York: Harcourt, Brace and Howe, 1919), Bartleby .com, 1999, www.bartleby.com/104/.

Chapter 4 We Are Not Alone

1. From the Good Friday liturgy in *The English Missal for the Laity* (London: W. Knott & Son Ltd., 1933).

Chapter 5 Love Is at Work in Our Broken World

1. Julian of Norwich, *Revelations of Divine Love* (London: Folio Society, 2017), 64–65.

2. J. R. R. Tolkien, *The Lord of the Rings*, Deluxe Illustrated Edition (New York: Houghton Mifflin, 1991), 894.

3. Tolkien, *The Lord of the Rings*, 900.

Incarnational Interlude

1. Tolkien, *The Lord of the Rings*, 988.

2. Wendell Berry, "Manifesto: The Mad Farmer's Liberation Front," in *The Selected Poems of Wendell Berry* (Berkeley, CA: Counterpoint, 1999).

Chapter 6 Refuge

1. David Bentley Hart, *The Beauty of the Infinite* (Grand Rapids: Eerdmans, 2003), 17.

2. Tolkien, *The Lord of the Rings*, 143.

3. Wendell Berry, *Hannah Coulter* (Washington, DC: Counterpoint, 2004), 67.

4. Berry, *Hannah Coulter*, 83.

5. Berry, *Hannah Coulter*, 158.

Chapter 7 Cadence and Celebration

1. C. S. Lewis, *The Discarded Image* (Cambridge: Cambridge University Press, 1964), 89.

2. Marilynne Robinson, *Lila* (London: Virago Press, 2014), 253.

3. Robinson, *Lila*, 135.

4. Thomas O'Loughlin, *Journeys on the Edges: The Celtic Tradition* (London: Darton, Longman and Todd Ltd., 2000), 39.

5. Thomas O'Loughlin, *Celtic Theology* (New York: Continuum, 2000), 128.

6. From the blessing "The Guiding Light of Eternity," in *The Carmina Gadelica*, https://www.sacred-texts.com/neu/celt/cg1/cg1014.htm.

7. Hans Boersma, *Heavenly Participation: The Weaving of a Sacramental Tapestry* (Grand Rapids: Eerdmans, 2011), 20.

8. Boersma, *Heavenly Participation*, 5.

9. Translation by Simon David Berry.

10. Madeleine L'Engle, *Walking on Water: Reflections on Faith & Art* (Colorado Springs: Waterbrook Press, 2001), 97.

Chapter 8 Fellowship

1. Robinson, *Lila*, 253.

2. See John 13:34.

3. J. K. Rowling, *Harry Potter and the Philosopher's Stone* (London: Bloomsbury, 1997), 299.

Chapter 9 Image

1. *The Secret of Kells*, directed by Tomm Moore (Cartoon Salon, 2009), animated film.

2. Richard Viladesau, *Theological Aesthetics* (New York: Oxford University Press, 1999), 16.

3. Kathleen L. Housley, "A Conversation with Jeremy Begbie," *Image Journal*, accessed December 15, 2020, https://www.imagejournal.org/article /a-conversation-with-jeremy-begbie/.

4. Tolkien, *The Lord of the Rings*, 957.

5. C. S. Lewis, "Tolkien's *The Lord of the Rings*," in *On Stories*, ed. Walter Hooper (Harvest Books, 2002), 89–90.

6. J. R. R. Tolkien, "On Fairy-Stories," in *Tree and Leaf* (London: Harper-Collins, 2012), 58.

7. C. S. Lewis, *Surprised by Joy: The Shape of My Early Life* (United Kingdom: HarperCollins, 1998), 18.

8. Owen Barfield, *Poetic Diction: A Study in Meaning* (Middletown, CT: Wesleyan University Press, 1984), 48.

9. Andrew Davison, ed., *Imaginative Apologetics* (Grand Rapids: Baker Academic, 2011), 15.

10. L'Engle, *Walking on Water*, 98.

11. Quoted by Dana Greene in *Denise Levertov: A Poet's Life* (Champaign, IL: University of Illinois Press, 2012), 71.

12. Willa Cather, *Song of the Lark* (New York: Barnes & Noble, 2008), 139.

13. L'Engle, *Walking on Water*, 10.

Chapter 10 Saint

1. From the poet Robert Frost's 1945 blank verse drama, "A Masque of Reason."

2. George Eliot, *Middlemarch* (United Kingdom: Bantam Books, 1985), 795.

3. Wendell Berry, *Remembering* (San Francisco: Northpoint Press, 1988), 58.

4. Berry, *Remembering*, 119.

5. David J. A. Clines, *Job 38–42*, vol. 18B of Word Biblical Commentary (Nashville: Thomas Nelson, 2011), 1202.

6. Denise Levertov, "Annunciation," in *A Door in the Hive* (New York: New Directions, 1989), 86.

Sarah Clarkson is an author and blogger who writes regularly about literature, faith, and beauty at www.sarahclarkson.com. She studied theology (BTh, MSt) at Oxford and is the author or coauthor of six books, including the recent *Book Girl*, a guide to the reading life. She has an active following on Instagram (@sarahwanders), where she hosts regular live read-alouds from the poems, novels, or essays that bring her courage. She can often be found with a cup of good tea and a book in hand in her home on the English coast, where she lives with her Anglican vicar husband, Thomas, and their two children, Lilian and Samuel.

CONNECT *with* SARAH

Sign up for Sarah Clarkson's newsletter and
find resources relating to *This Beautiful Truth* at

sarahclarkson.com

@sarahwanders   @saraheclarkson   @thoroughlyalive

LIKE THIS
BOOK?

Consider sharing it with others!

- Share or mention the book on your social media platforms. Use the hashtag **#ThisBeautifulTruth**.

- Write a book review on your blog or on a retailer site.

- Pick up a copy for friends, family, or anyone who you think would enjoy and be challenged by its message!

- Share this message on Twitter, Facebook, or Instagram: I loved **#ThisBeautifulTruth** by @sarahwanders // @ReadBakerBooks

- Recommend this book for your church, workplace, book club, or class.

- Follow Baker Books on social media and tell us what you like.

 ReadBakerBooks

 ReadBakerBooks

 ReadBakerBooks